Fitting a Camper Van Interior

Fitting a Camper Van Interior

Rob Hawkins

THE CROWOOD PRESS

First published in 2014 by
The Crowood Press Ltd
Ramsbury, Marlborough
Wiltshire SN8 2HR

www.crowood.com

British Library Cataloguing-in-Publication Data
A catalogue record for this book is available from the British Library.

ISBN 978 1 84797 605 5

Photography by Rob Hawkins, unless otherwise stated.

Typeset by Jean Cussons Typesetting, Diss, Norfolk

Printed and bound in India by Replika Press Pvt Ltd

contents

designing and planning an interior

Before you get stuck into making an interior for a camper van, there are several points to consider first. This chapter deals with choosing the right vehicle for a camper-van conversion and assessing whether it needs modifying to cope with the extra load. There is guidance on deciding what equipment to fit and where it should be fitted, plus the materials that can be used, where to find them and the necessary tools for making an interior.

price of these increasingly collectible and popular classics also puts people off, when they realize they can get a lot for their money by purchasing something that may not be quite so appealing, but it will provide daily transport and accommodation for holidays.

If you haven't already bought a van you intend to convert and equip with a camper van interior, then research

the subject thoroughly. If you intend to buy second-hand, use websites such as Autotrader, who have a van section at www.Autotrader.co.uk for the UK and equivalent websites in other countries. Also check club websites for specific models. Find out how much particular vans are selling for and whether there are any specific models that demand a higher or lower price. A turbo diesel

CHOOSE YOUR VEHICLE

There are so many different vans and dedicated camper vans this book applies to, ranging from the classic VW Split Screen and later Bay Window to the modern Japanese Hiace from Toyota, the Mercedes Sprinter and Ford Transit. Many people would like to have a classic camper van, but are dissuaded by rumours of unreliability, lack of modern equipment and slowing everyone down on country lanes. The

The modern VW Bay Window is powered by a 1.4-litre water cooled VW Polo engine, making it more economical, reliable and marginally faster than the original.

The elevating roof on the Mazda Bongo is standard on many models and includes a sleeping compartment, saving thousands on a pop-top conversion.

engine VW T25, for instance, often sells for more than an air-cooled equivalent because it is more economical, returning around 40mpg (7ltr/100km) instead of 20–25mpg (14–11ltr/100km).

Which van you choose should be based on a number of factors. Compare the standard specification of different vans to see what you get for your money. For example, many Mazda Bongos already have an electronic elevating roof as standard, with a sleeping compartment for two, pull down blinds, rear heating and seating for eight people that folds down into a double bed, enabling four people to sleep inside the van. These features could cost over £4,000 to fit to some vans, but they are already fitted to most Bongos.

Whilst the Mazda Bongo has camping features fitted during its manufacture, there are a number of vans and minibuses that have been professionally converted into camper vans by the likes of Danbury and Westfalia. Buying such a camper van often means there is already an elevating roof, cupboards, curtains and a kitchen. Such conversions often demand a higher second-hand price.

If you are intending to purchase a standard van with no rear interior and convert it yourself, consider how much space is available, whether the front seats can be converted to swivel round and face the rear, and if access to the rear is possible from the front – some vans have a bulkhead behind the front seats that's a structural part of the van, so it cannot be removed.

It's always worthwhile comparing the cost of buying a particular camper van and the equivalent standard van that hasn't been converted. The standard unconverted van should be a lot

cheaper, but carefully consider the cost of a conversion to the same specification. The van may have been used as daily transport with the minimum amount of maintenance, whereas a camper van will probably have less mileage and abuse.

Maintenance is an important point that can be difficult to fully appreciate when purchasing a camper van. Whether you intend to service and repair the vehicle yourself or not, find out the full details of servicing. Modern van engines may have a timing

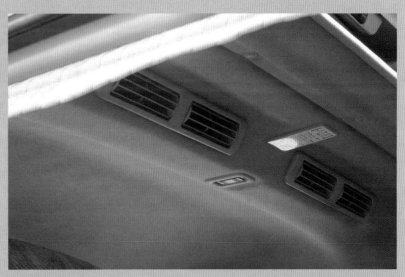

This roof-mounted rear heater in a Mazda Bongo is a standard feature on most vehicles.

Buying a standard van, such as this VW T5, may be a lot cheaper than buying the same age of camper van, but the cost of the conversion to the same standard may result in total costs being a lot more.

TOP LEFT: Classic VW vans, such as the Split Screen and this Bay Window, have an engine in the rear, which is relatively straightforward to access and maintain.

BELOW LEFT: The Mazda Bongo is well known for head-gasket failure, but it's often caused by neglecting to check the coolant pipe that's attached to the engine.

BELOW RIGHT: Access to the Mazda Bongo engine is via the front seats that tilt backwards, but if an interior is fitted, they have to be removed.

belt that needs to be changed every 40,000 miles (64,000km), for instance – find out how much this will cost to do and whether you can do it yourself. All engines require general servicing, such as oil and filters, so find out how much serviceable items cost and whether you can fit them yourself. There are some big differences. The air-cooled petrol engines found in many classic VW camper vans, such as Split Screens, Bay Windows and some T25s, take a matter of minutes to drain the oil, clean the strainer and top up with 2–3ltr of new oil. Changing the oil on the Mazda Bongo will take much longer, requiring the front seats to be tilted back or removed to access the oil filter, filler cap and dipstick.

Look into the typical mechanical, electrical or other problems associated with the van you want to buy. Find out how these problems are fixed and if they can be fixed quickly should they arise during a holiday. In some cases, common problems can be eliminated through regular maintenance. The Bongo for instance, has a reputation for head-gasket failure, but this is often

caused by a hose between the engine and radiator perishing and leaking. The hose should be checked at every service interval and renewed if it has deteriorated. A similar problem exists on diesel engine T25s, where the radiator is at the front and the engine is at the rear. If the cooling system is not routinely checked and parts renewed, then it will fail and overheat the engine.

However, there are a number of known problems with some camper vans that simply require a stock of spare parts and tools to be kept on board. Spare spark plugs, HT leads, points, con-

densers and clutch and throttle cables should always be stored inside every air-cooled VW camper van, for instance.

Another aspect that's just as important as maintenance concerns the drivability of a camper van. Consider how you want to use it and how frequently it will need to be used. Do you want to use it as daily transport or lock it away for the winter and tax it for six months of the year? When it's used, do you need to get to destinations as quickly as possible, or are you happy to take your time? There's a big difference between driving a classic camper

This radiator from a water-cooled VW T25 sits at the front of the vehicle, whereas the engine is at the rear. If the cooling system is neglected, it could leak and the engine will overheat.

This Toyota Hiace has modern controls and power steering that will make a trip down to the south of France seem effortless.

Driving comforts in a classic VW, such as this Bay Window, are limited, but the experience is part of the trip.

van that may struggle to reach 60mph (100km/h) and a modern van that will cruise all day through Europe at 80mph (130km/h). There's also the cost implication of travel. A classic VW camper van may return 25mpg (11ltr/100km), whereas a modern diesel engine van can return twice as much. A holiday involving 1,000 miles of travel can result in a huge difference in fuel costs – 40 gallons (182ltr) of fuel for a classic camper van versus 20 (90ltr) for a modern diesel.

There is a noticeable difference between a classic camper van and a modern one when driving. Speed, acceleration, noise, steering and ride comfort are all completely different. Driving a classic camper van has to be part of the holiday and be regarded as a nostalgic experience. A modern camper van is more convenient.

One of the most important considerations when buying a camper van, or a van to convert, is the subject of headroom. It can be one of the biggest expenses to convert, so requires lots of thought and research into what you

It may look nostalgic, but running a classic camper van requires preparation, patience and lots of maintenance.

want. The headroom height of most camper vans falls into three categories. At the basic level, there's what's known as the tin top – a low-level roof that cannot be raised. The second option is an elevating roof, which rises up and forms a tent on the top of the camper van; there's not only room to stand up, but space to add a couple of beds. This is a popular choice because it can be

folded down when driving, thus reducing the height of the vehicle and allowing entry into car parks with height restrictions.

The third category is a fixed high top. Some vans are sufficiently high as standard (e.g. the Ford Transit high top), but many others require a hole to be cut in the roof and a taller GRP roof to be fitted. The advantage of such a setup

An elevating roof is ideal for adding extra sleeping space and headroom when cooking. Plus, it folds down, allowing the van to fit in to most garages.

A fixed high-top roof provides extra storage and sleeping space and headroom. There's also less of a risk of leaks over a pop-top.

is permanent space, allowing extra storage in the roof along with the benefits of beds and headroom. The disadvantages of a high top include not being able to access car parks with height restriction barriers and being battered by side winds on the motorway.

CONTENTS CHECKLIST

It's far too easy to become carried away with what you would like to have inside a camper van. Space is generally limited, so the following section helps you to decide whether a toilet, shower and flat-screen television are really necessary.

A good starting point for designing an interior is to consider how many people are going to need to use it and for what purpose. Seating is one of the most important aspects, so make sure you can accommodate everyone that will, or may need to, travel inside the camper van. Additional seating can be created by fitting a bench seat at the

front for three people, for example. A full-width rock-and-roll bed in the rear can also seat three people.

When considering how many people you may need to transport in your camper van, also think about the amount of weight you will be carrying, especially with older, less powerful vehicles. Six adults for instance, can weigh almost half a ton if each adult weighs an average of 75kg or roughly 11 stone 10lbs.

Sleeping arrangements are just as important as seating, although they are a little more flexible with awnings and tents. A full-width rock-and-roll bed can usually accommodate two adults and a small child, but if you need plenty of storage space, you may want to fit a narrower ¾ size rock-and-roll bed and fit wardrobes and cupboards alongside. Bunks can be fitted in pop-tops and high top roofs. A hammock can be fitted across the front seats (*see* Chapter 4 for a step-by-step guide).

Once you have decided upon the seating and sleeping criteria, the next stage is to plan a list of camping essentials. The basics may include a cool box, cooker and cupboards for food, crockery, cutlery and clothes. However, the list can easily expand with a fridge, table, rear-facing buddy seat, electrics, lighting and sink. If you've camped with a tent before, especially with children, you can appreciate how much equipment you often need. Squeezing all of this into a camper van is feasible, but you need to source the correct components and be ruthless with what you actually require.

Space and weight are two major factors that will restrict how much can be fitted inside a camper van. So consider whether you can manage without some equipment. A sink with water tanks for fresh and waste water, for example, can take up a lot of space and will add a lot of weight. One litre of water weighs one kilo, so even if you limit the water to a modest 10ltr, that's still 10kg that needs to be secured somewhere inside or underneath the camper van.

Deciding where everything can be fitted will help to determine what you can feasibly fit inside the camper van. Think long and hard about how you can use specific equipment. For instance, can you stand up when cooking or will you need to sit down (in which case, you'll need a seat near the cooker)? When cooking, can you access the cupboards for the crockery, cutlery and food and also the fridge or cool box?

Similar considerations need to be made if you intend to fit a table for dining. Most camper van tables are small and only suitable for two or three

A bench seat up front can often accommodate three people.

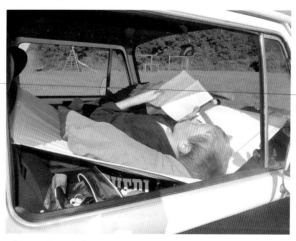

A hammock can be fitted across the front seats and is suitable for a child.

This three-quarter size rock-and-roll bed is suitable for two people and allows storage compartments to be fitted alongside.

Cooking in a camper van can be a logistical nightmare if there's no room to stand or sit, or to access the cupboards and fridge.

Fitted wardrobes and cupboards don't take up much space inside this Ford Transit van, but when fitted inside a smaller classic VW, for example, light and elbow room are soon lost.

people to sit around. You may have to consider fitting additional tables.

Storage space for clothes and other items you need to carry is one of the most difficult aspects of designing a camper van interior. You can never have enough storage space, but squeezing lots of wardrobes, overhead lockers and cupboards into a camper van can have its problems, including additional weight, less room to manoeuvre and less light. It's hard to do, but it's worthwhile trying to calculate how much space you really need for all the aforementioned items, then looking around the inside of your van to see where they can be stored.

WEIGHT ISSUES

It's difficult to appreciate the accumulative weight of clothes, a table, tins of food and crockery, and what effect they can have on driving your camper van, but this is one aspect that needs some careful consideration for several reasons.

If you use household kitchen worktops and cupboards to construct the interior of your camper van, the weight of these is very heavy when compared to the lighter materials shown in this book and the materials used by professional converters. So in many cases, it's important to source lightweight materials, which is covered later in this chapter.

The positioning of large objects will affect the camper van's stability under cornering and could be dangerous in the event of an accident. An overhead locker that's crammed full of food tins

and other heavy objects can increase body roll under cornering and become a lethal missile in the event of an accident if it and its contents are not sufficiently secure. Overhead storage is useful, but the materials used to construct a cupboard need to be light, along with the items that are stored inside it.

This retro-looking furniture is heavy and robust, adding unwanted weight to the overall van.

A heavy overhead cupboard can add top-heavy weight to a van, which affects the handling of the vehicle under cornering.

Fitting a performance air-filter should help the engine breathe better and provide a more responsive throttle.

A performance exhaust system can help to make an engine livelier, but make sure it isn't too loud.

IS YOUR CAMPER VAN UP TO THE JOB?

Extra weight on board is more of a problem for classic camper vans, especially when they are being driven on the road. The additional load means the engine has to work harder, so acceleration may be slower. Reducing the weight of the contents can help, but you may have to consider modifying the engine to produce a little more power to help climb hills and maintain a cruising speed.

Most engines can be mildly tuned with a performance air-filter, which should help improve airflow and provide a better throttle response. If your camper van has a panel-shaped air-filter, manufacturers such as K&N and Pipercross may produce a replacement filter for around £20–30. Otherwise, an open cone-shaped air-filter can probably be fitted either in the form of a specific kit or a universal kit consisting of appropriate pipework. The most expensive performance air-filters

This classic VW air-cooled engine has been modified with twin carburettors for better fuelling and a performance coil for a more reliable spark.

are closed-air systems, comprising an air-filter inside a canister with a cold air feed pipe. This is the most effective setup, but can cost over £200 for a made to measure kit.

Don't expect masses of extra power from a performance air-filter, but it should make the engine a little more driveable and most filters are reusable (they require washing), so after several years they will be cheaper than a disposable filter.

Tuning boxes can help modern diesel and petrol engines to perform better.

A performance air-filter will be of more benefit if other engine modifications are incorporated, such as a free-flowing exhaust system, which helps the engine breathe more freely. Depending on your camper van and its engine, there are a wide range of specialist exhaust systems and silencers that can help. When shopping around, be aware that some systems will generate extra noise. If you want the exhaust noise to be kept to a minimum, look for quiet-pack exhaust systems.

A popular and effective upgrade on many classic petrol engine camper vans is to change the carburettors. Many of the classic VW Split Screens and Bay Windows have a single carburettor, but this can be changed for either a larger single carburettor or two of them. Budget for between £200 and £400 for this modification, which many people regard as money well spent.

There are several engine components that can be uprated to help make sure they remain reliable, especially when the engine is being revved hard to overtake or drive up a hill. An electronic ignition conversion with a high-performance coil, better HT leads and spark plugs will all help and are relatively straightforward to fit.

Even if you have a modern camper van with a strong diesel engine, some of the aforementioned upgrades can be fitted (air-filter and exhaust) to help provide a smoother delivery of power and improve performance. Tuning boxes are also popular, which alter the programming of the engine control unit (ECU) by altering the fuelling. Many can improve the pulling power of an engine as well as making it more economical. Budget for between £200 and £400 for a tuning box.

Whilst improving an engine's performance may help to compensate for the extra load taken on board with a camper van conversion, the brakes and suspension are also working harder. Routine maintenance will ensure the brakes are working to the best of their ability. On disc brakes, make sure the brake pads are not sticking – remove and clean their edges and around where they sit. Modern disc brakes feature sliders to operate the outer brake pad, which should be free to move in and out.

Servicing the brakes will ensure they are working to the best of their ability.

Some camper vans may require heavy duty springs and dampers to cope with the additional weight of a conversion.

If you want better brakes for your camper van, look into cheap and straightforward modifications, such as better brake pads and braided steel flexi-hoses before spending lots of money on performance brake kits. Simple upgrades, such as fitting ducting to direct cool air to the brakes and prevent them getting too hot under harsh braking, can make a big difference.

The suspension has to work harder when it is carrying additional loads, so you may want to fit heavy-duty springs and dampers. If the vehicle has been lowered, the tyres may catch the arches, so the ride height will need to be raised.

TESTING AND RESEARCH

It's very difficult to visualize the best way to construct the interior of a camper van. Ideas often fail due to a lack of space or unforeseen problems, so the best way to discover whether they are feasible is to mock them up and test them. For instance, if you would like the front seats to swivel around to face each other, allowing a table to be fitted in the middle and two people to eat at it, start by sitting two people in this position. You may find there isn't the legroom to do this, but luckily you have only spent a few minutes finding this out.

Some testing isn't so easy, such as seeing if an assortment of fitted cupboards and wardrobes would block out too much light and make the interior look cramped. In such a situation, use various sizes of cardboard box to act as dummy furniture.

Seating arrangements are one of the hardest aspects of a camper van, especially when it comes to food preparation and dining. However, there are some cheap methods of testing, involving a fold-away picnic table and boxes to sit on instead of seats. Such a setup allows you to move things around and try different seating arrangements.

One of the most helpful ways of working out how best to create an interior for a camper van is to visit a show. Here you will find lots of examples of other people's work, what equipment they have fitted, the materials they have used and the problems they have

discovered. Opinions are always mixed, so be prepared to become bewildered.

DESIGN ON PAPER

Once you have formulated your ideas as to the layout and contents you want incorporated into your camper van, don't solely rely upon a plan in your head. Take measurements to find out whether a fridge, cooker and rock-and-roll bed will all fit in their respective locations. Draw an overhead plan of different layouts, and include measurements to calculate how much space you will have to work with. You may discover that a cupboard alongside a fridge isn't large enough to fit a cereal box inside or store a water container. Such problems are best identified at this stage.

MATERIALS

The materials you will need to construct a camper van interior can be very expensive or extremely cheap, depending on whether you are willing to shop around and look at a variety of sources.

The raw materials used for making your own work surfaces, bunk beds and seats vary in price and weight.

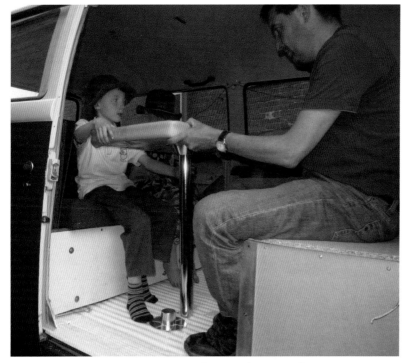

Trial fitting a table helps to see where it should be fitted and whether a rear-facing seat (wooden box on the right) would be of benefit.

Camper van related shows are a good source of research to see what other people have fitted in their own vehicles.

As a general rule, the heavier the material, the cheaper it is, but that is not always the case. The following points outline some of the most useful materials available and what they can be used for.

◆ Aluminium: Aluminium is strong and lightweight, but sadly not very cheap. However, most metal stockists sell offcuts, which can be used to create a camper van interior. Angled aluminium is useful for making mounts or fixing panels together. Sheet aluminium can be used for doors and worktops.

◆ Plywood: This lightweight wood is available in different thicknesses and is ideal for doors, worktops, shelves and interior panels. It's cheap to buy from most DIY stores and easy to cut. It can be painted to produce a professional finish.

◆ Flexible plywood: Whilst standard plywood is rigid, flexible plywood can bend in one or two directions, making it ideal for curved sections, such as an overhead locker. It's more expensive than standard plywood.

◆ Medium-density fibreboard (MDF): A popular and cheap material that's easy to work with, cheaper than plywood, but heavy. Ideal for seat bases, cupboard doors and other rigid panels.

◆ Hardboard: Lightweight and useful for adding a finish to a panel. Available in a coloured gloss finish, as well as brown. Suitable for interior panels and covering a seatboard. Moderately flexible and can be cut with a knife.

◆ Vinyl wrap: Tatty or cheap-looking panels can be quickly revived with vinyl. This self-adhesive material is available in a variety of patterns and colours. *See* Chapter 3 for a series of step-by-step guides on fitting vinyl to panels.

This aluminium tread plate was purchased as an offcut from a metal supplier and cost £25. It can be used as a kitchen worktop.

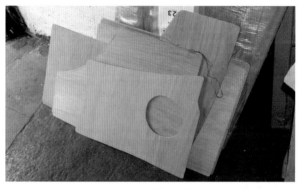

Plywood is cheap to buy, available in different thicknesses and easy to cut to shape.

Curved panels can be constructed from flexible plywood, which can bend in one or two directions.

MDF is heavy, but cheap and useful for seat bases and other rigid panels.

Hardboard is cheap, flexible and easy to cut. A painted finish is useful for covering old panels.

Covering a panel in vinyl can transform its appearance.

LEFT: *Unwanted household furniture is a cheap source of materials, but can be heavy.*

ABOVE: *Old caravans can be found on eBay and often cost less than a brand new camper van fridge.*

A second-hand rock-and-roll bed found inside a camper van in a breakers yard may prove to be a bargain find.

The seats, trim and electrics from a scrap car can all be used in a camper van.

SOURCING PARTS

Camper van and camping specialists are some of the best sources of parts, but a lot of the general equipment you may require can be found elsewhere as well. Cupboard door hinges, door locks and trim can be found at a variety of outlets ranging from caravan manufacturers to general DIY shops, for instance. The following points highlight some ideas for collecting parts from alternative sources.

◆ Old furniture: Household furniture, such as kitchen cupboard doors, an old wardrobe or sideboard can be used to construct a camper van interior. However, the materials used are often heavy, so look for lightweight pine, not thick and heavy chipboard.
◆ Abandoned caravan: An old cara-

van can be bought for less than the price of a camper van fridge and often has a lot of the equipment and materials you will need. There are also caravan scrapyards, which won't be as cheap as buying a caravan to strip yourself, but will allow you to buy only the items you need.
◆ Scrapyard vans: There are several breakers yards that specialize in vans or camper vans, where a second-hand pop-top for instance, can be bought, an old rock-and-roll bed or a complete Devon interior.
◆ Scrap cars: Breakers yards for cars are a cheap source for battery terminals, rubber seals, trim, seats and other car parts that can be used in a camper van.

USEFUL TOOLS

Depending on the extent of the work

you plan to do on your camper van, the list of tools may be very basic, such as a saw for cutting wood and a screwdriver for fitting a kitchen unit together. However, this book covers an extensive range of step-by-step guides, showing how to fit everything from a leisure battery to a pop-top roof. A comprehensive list of every possible tool wouldn't really be of interest, and each step-by-step guide includes a tool list anyway, so the following list outlines some of the tools that have proven to be the most useful when making your own camper van interior.

◆ Staple gun: Useful for attaching upholstery to the underside of a wooden board. Budget for £8–10 plus a few packs of staples.
◆ Drill: Variable-speed battery-operated drill is ideal for drilling holes and fitting screws.

◆ Jigsaw: Useful for quickly cutting straight and shaped pieces of wood. Can also be used for cutting out windows in a panel van and even a hole in the roof for a pop-top or high-top conversion.

◆ Pop rivet gun: Useful for quickly securing metal brackets and panels in position. Drill a suitable hole (4–5mm usually), fit a pop rivet and squeeze it together with a gun.

◆ Rivet nut tool: If you need to fit a threaded hole into a panel to secure a bolt, a rivet nut does the job. The tool is similar to a pop rivet gun.

◆ Angle grinder: Armed with a cutting disc, an angle grinder can cleanly cut through sheet aluminium to help create the correct-sized panels. Also useful for cutting holes for windows and a pop-top or high-top conversion.

A staple gun can quickly secure upholstery to the underside of a seat base or trim panel.

Time-saving battery-operated drill can make holes and fit screws.

Shape wooden panels with a jigsaw. Use a metal blade to cut out windows.

Fix panels quickly with a pop rivet gun.

Make your own threaded holes for fitting bolts by using a rivet nut tool.

Slice through sheet aluminium with an angle grinder equipped with a cutting disc.

safety issues

This is probably the one chapter that most readers skip through or bypass. It covers the subjects whose consequences you don't really want to suffer, whether it's a fire, an accident or injury either during the creation of your camper van's interior or whilst camping. However, the best way of preventing such catastrophes is, first of all, to read this chapter and, second, to be proactive. So this chapter outlines many of the best ways of working to avoid disasters and what you can incorporate in your camper van to help prevent fires and accidents.

WHAT CAN GO WRONG?

There are a number of potential disasters that can occur during the creation of your camper van's interior, whilst you are driving the vehicle and using it for camping. The more you are aware of these possible problems, the better equipped you will be to avoid them. Many of the potential problems require knowledge of how your camper van is constructed and how particular components work. You may not have that knowledge, but the necessary information can always be found.

Electrics

A camper van's electrics can be extremely complicated or very simple, but in all cases, you need to have at least a basic understanding of how equipment is operated and where the fuses, relay switches and wiring are located should a problem occur.

The biggest problem with a camper van's electrics concerns fires, which is

covered in greater detail later in this chapter. However, there are other less disastrous problems, such as blown fuses and equipment that doesn't work.

A good starting point for electrics when it comes to a camper van is to know where the fuse box or boxes are located. Most camper vans usually have them located in the engine bay or underneath the dashboard. When you have found them, look for any dia-

Find out where all of the fuses are located and make sure you have a range of spares.

grams that help identify the fuses and make sure you have the correct spares. Fuses are rated according to amps, so they are usually labelled with a number, such as 10 that represents 10 amps.

Problems concerning dodgy wiring, poor earths and faulty equipment can often start with a blown fuse, so it's essential to know where the fuses are and how to change them. Tracing these problems can often take time, so ensure you have some knowledge of your camper van's wiring and how components should be correctly connected, especially if they are using power from the vehicle's battery or a leisure battery. Equipment such as a multimeter and socket tester can help to identify problems concerning wiring where, for example, there's no supply of voltage to a switch because the wire to it has broken down.

If you intend to complete the wiring in your camper van to be able to connect to main electricity, for instance, and use a leisure battery, then make sure you have a thorough knowledge of how components need to be fitted and correctly wired. Fuses are essential to reduce the risk of melted wires and burnt-out equipment. Similarly, relay switches must be fitted in most situations where equipment draws a large amount of current, but requires a manual switch to turn it on and off. If you are at all unsure about how camper van electrics should be correctly fitted, seek professional advice.

Gas and Gases

There are a number of safety rules to adhere to when it comes to fitting gas appliances. Most camper vans use butane for gas cookers, fridges, heaters and hot water. The gas is stored in a

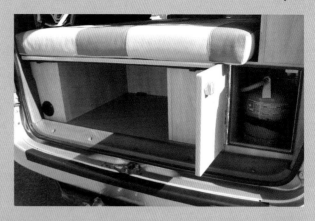

A gas bottle must be securely stored and adequately ventilated. Some countries stipulate that it must be stored in a fireproof cabinet.

This portable gas stove is a popular camping accessory and uses a disposable canister, which must be detached when not in use.

GAS BOTTLE REGULATIONS

The laws surrounding fitting a gas bottle inside a camper van vary from country to country. In some cases they must be fitted by a qualified professional, stored in a fireproof cabinet and regularly checked. Find out what you need to do before fitting one.

---

bottle, which must be securely located inside the camper van to help prevent the risk of it moving in the event of an accident and causing injury or damage. The area in which the gas bottle is secured must be ventilated to ensure the gas can leave the van if it leaks out of the gas bottle. Most camper vans have a vent hole in the floor, as butane is heavier than air, so it will sink.

The waste gases produced by gas-operated appliances, such as a cooker, fridge or heater, also need to be properly ventilated to reduce the risk of poisonous fumes filling the interior. These gases, especially carbon monoxide, are often slightly lighter than air, but may get mixed with warm rising air. Consequently, there are different recommendations for ventilation according to the type of equipment being fitted. Gas-powered fridges, for example, often have an outside vent fitted at the height of the fridge or slightly higher. However, such equipment should have instructions on where a vent must be fitted. If equipment isn't suitable for

use in a camper van, such as a portable fridge that should only be operated on gas when the fridge is outside, do not connect it to a gas bottle when it is installed inside the camper van.

When it comes to cooking, the waste gases produced must also be removed from inside the camper van, so leaving a door or window open when cooking is essential. However, it may be tempting to warm the interior of the camper van when cooking or even lighting a gas ring on the stove to produce some heat. It generally only takes a few minutes to warm up an interior, which is usually insufficient to create an excessive amount of waste gases. Leaving a gas stove burning all night on a low heat is, however, dangerous. Similarly, placing a smouldering disposable barbecue inside the camper van to create heat throughout the night is equally dangerous.

The connections to a gas bottle must be secure and leak-free. A cut-off valve (regulator) should be fitted on top of the gas bottle to ensure you can switch

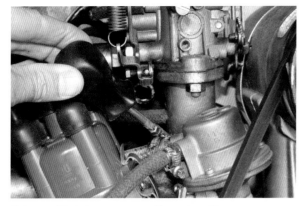

Make sure all fuel pipes are secure and in good condition.

This dried-up windscreen seal will undoubtedly let water through and may leak onto any electrics inside the camper van.

off the gas. Any pipework from the gas bottle must be of the approved type, which in most cases is rubber with a diameter of 8mm. Do not use any type of pipe; it must be specifically for gas-operated camping equipment.

There are a number of gas stoves that use small and compact canisters instead of a gas bottle. These must be treated in the same manner as a large gas bottle, ensuring they are safely stored away when not in use and, if possible, isolated or detached from their appliance. The same risk of waste gases applies to these smaller stoves.

Leaks

There can be a range of fluids kept on board a camper van, which can result in a variety of problems if they escape. Fuel leaks are one of the biggest threats on older camper vans, so it's essential to ensure all fuel pipes are in good condition. Leaking fuel can not only result in an engine fire, the fumes can fill the interior, especially in older VW camper vans where the fuel tank, pipework and engine are all in the rear of the vehicle.

Water is one of the biggest liquid-based enemies of a camper van. Even if you do not have fresh and waste water stored inside the camper van, rain-water can leak through a poorly sealed pop-top and old window seals. If the water seeps through to the electrics, it can result in blown fuses and electrical failure. Long-term trouble includes corrosion, where the water rots the metal bodywork of the camper van.

The best way to avoid water leaking into the camper van is to know where it can get in and make sure these areas are as water-tight as possible. Renew window and pop-top seals if they are old and, if this still doesn't help, make sure any water that does get through doesn't settle on any electrics. You may have to resort to frequently checking for water leaks and drying them, so make sure the affected areas are adequately rustproofed.

Flying Objects

A camper van's interior is designed to be packed with food, sleeping bags, clothes and people, so it's essential all

of these items can be securely contained, especially when the vehicle is moving. Cupboard doors need to have secure locking mechanisms that can withstand the impact of the objects they are concealing. A magnetic latch on a cupboard door, for example, may be useless if there are several tins of baked beans behind it. This is a similar problem on some fridges where a plastic lock will break if all the food inside pushes against the door under heavy braking or cornering.

The location of items inside a camper van is also an important consideration, especially if they escape. A battery-operated LED light, for instance, may only weigh a few grams and can seem perfectly secure stuck onto the inside of the camper van with a magnet. However, in the event of an accident, it can become extremely dangerous if it becomes airborne and could easily fly through the windscreen or, even worse, injure someone.

Making sure everything is secure inside a camper van isn't an easy task and the starting point is often at the design stage of the interior, where the

Locks for cupboard doors and fridges must be able to withstand the impact of the items behind them.

Lightweight items should be stored in the upper-half of the camper van to help reduce the risk of it becoming too top heavy.

location of cupboards and other storage needs to be carefully planned. It's also important to plan the weight distribution of clothes, sleeping bags and other essentials. Filling an overhead locker full of food tins, for instance, is not only potentially dangerous in the event of an accident, it also adds to the weight at the top of the camper van, making it more top-heavy. It has a similar effect to adding luggage to a roof rack, resulting in extra weight on the top, which becomes more of a handful under cornering.

The distribution of weight is an important consideration that is often difficult to appreciate. The weight of seats, beds, kitchen pods, gas bottles, water storage and people can almost double the original weight of the camper van. If more of this weight is biased to one side or corner of the vehicle, then the handling and braking will be affected, especially under extreme circumstances. Try to keep the majority of the weight low down and evenly distributed.

MAINTENANCE DRILLS

It is essential to devise a list of routine checks that should be conducted at frequent intervals, whether it is every time the camper van is used or at the start, middle and end of every season. The following steps outline some of the points to consider.

1   Engine checks: Make sure you can easily access the engine and run through some routine checks of the oil, coolant, power-steering fluid and brake fluid. Accessing the engine may be difficult, but it's essential to know it's in good working order.
2   Wheel nuts and tyres: The only thing keeping you in contact with the tarmac is the tyres, so make sure they are correctly inflated and are not worn to the limit. Also, periodically check that the wheel nuts are sufficiently tight.
3   Lifting pop-tops: If your camper van has a pop-top, always check it is securely strapped down before a journey. Some pop-tops have internal and external locking mechanisms, so check all of these are in place.

Regularly check the engine oil and other fluids, even if access is awkward, such as on this Mazda Bongo.

Invest in a torque wrench and correctly tighten the wheel nuts for peace of mind.

Pop-tops are often secured from the inside and outside, so regularly check the fastenings.

TOP LEFT: *Frequently check exterior luggage is secure throughout a journey.*

BELOW LEFT: *Regularly check all appliances work properly. Fridges need to be run at frequent intervals.*

BELOW RIGHT: *Keep batteries topped up and make sure their connections are secure.*

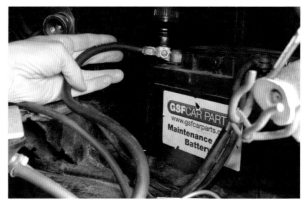

4 Exterior luggage: Camper vans are ideal for carrying bikes on the back and luggage on the roof, but make sure you know how to secure these items correctly, and regularly stop during a journey to check them.

5 Gas and electrics: Make sure there's sufficient gas before a holiday and test all appliances. Before a journey, switch off the gas and make sure appliances, such as the fridge, are correctly set.

6 Batteries: Make sure the battery or batteries are fully charged and securely connected. Camper vans may have long periods of inactivity, so disconnect the batteries and recharge them, if necessary.

WORK TOOLS AND PROTECTION

An assortment of tools are required to make a camper van interior, many of which can be dangerous if they are used incorrectly, such as electric drills and angle grinders. It's essential not only to know how to operate this equipment, but to wear appropriate clothing to protect you. When using an angle grinder, metal sparks and debris will fly in all directions, so make sure you are wearing a suitable pair of goggles, thick gloves and that most of your body is covered in clothing. Hot sparks can drop into your clothing, so wear a jacket with a tight collar.

Grinding sparks can also damage the camper van, especially glass and upholstery, so protect it with thick blankets or cardboard.

If you need to weld, the same rules apply as using an angle grinder, except you will need a suitable welding mask to avoid damaging your eyes – make sure there is nobody nearby who could look at the light created when welding and potentially damage their eyesight.

It's highly probable you will need to drill lots of holes when fitting a camper van interior, which entails the use of

Sparks generated from an angle grinder can damage upholstery and glass, so make sure it is protected.

MIG welding can damage your eyesight, so make sure you wear a suitable mask.

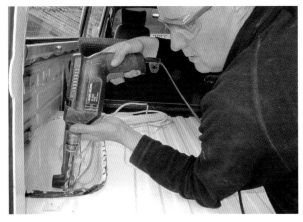

Always wear safety goggles when drilling holes to avoid debris hitting your eyes.

an electric drill, whether it is mains or battery-operated. Few people admit to wearing goggles when drilling, unless a piece of debris has flicked up from the rotating drill bit and hit them in the eye. It can easily happen, so always wear goggles.

There will probably be a number of materials or areas of the camper van that require painting. Make sure paint is applied in a well-ventilated area and left to fully dry. The fumes generated from some paints can be hazardous, especially for anyone with respiratory problems. Similarly, if you are rubbing down old paintwork, wear a mask if you have breathing problems or are unsure of what the old paint contains.

Paint fumes can be dangerous, so always apply it in a well-ventilated area.

FIRE-FIGHTING EQUIPMENT

Nobody wants seriously to consider what you should do in the event of a fire, unless you have experienced it already. When it comes to a fire in a camper van, it's all too easy to assume such a fire would be relatively simple to extinguish, but there are many situations where this is not the case. Camp-

er vans are often packed with the sort of materials and chemicals that easily cause fires, so planning how to deal with a fire is very important.

There are a number of different pieces of equipment that can help to put out fires, alert you to fires and help when a fire is underway. The following ten steps outline some of the popular choices and some of the important points that need to be considered to help avoid fires.

1   Having one or two fire-extinguishers inside the camper van is essential, providing they can easily be accessed and operated should a fire start. Some fire-extinguishers are supplied with a cage, which can be mounted onto a panel. Make sure there is no risk of the fire-extinguisher falling out of the cage, especially during heavy braking.

CLEANING UP

Find out how to clean up after using a fire-extinguisher and whether any special cleaning products are required. If, for example, you use a fire-extinguisher on an engine fire, you need to know whether the engine can be run afterwards and how to remove the foam or powder expelled from the fire-extinguisher.

Most handheld fire-extinguishers are straightforward to secure inside the camper van using a mounting cage.

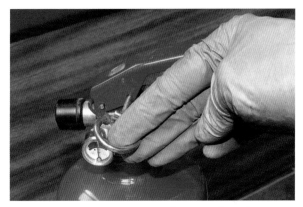

Make sure you know how to operate your fire-extinguisher – it's no use waiting until there is a fire.

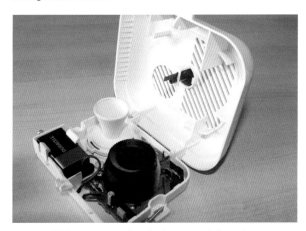

A household, battery-operated smoke detector can help to alert you to a fire.

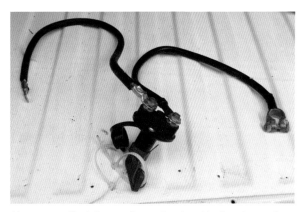

A battery cut-off switch can make sure there is nothing live when you leave your camper van, helping to reduce the risk of fire.

RIGHT: Automatic fire-extinguishers are activated upon heat and are useful if there's space to fit one inside an engine bay.

BELOW: A fire blanket can quickly starve a fire of oxygen and help to put it out. It's useful for cooking fires.

2 Automatic fire-extinguishers are a useful addition to a handheld, manual fire-extinguisher. Most of them feature a temperature bubble, which bursts and activates the fire-extinguisher if the surrounding temperature exceeds a specific value (e.g. 80°C).

3 Make sure you know how to operate your fire-extinguisher, whether there is any method of checking its level and if it needs to be refilled. Some fire-extinguishers have a pressure gauge as a level indicator. Also, check whether the fire-extinguisher has an expiry date.

4 Another method of extinguishing a fire is to use a fire-blanket. This is less messy than an extinguisher and useful for chemical fires (e.g. cooking oil and petrol) where a blanket can effectively starve the fire of oxygen and put it out.

5 A smoke-detector can help to identify a fire when it starts and could save valuable seconds in being able to put it out quickly. Household, battery-operated smoke-detectors can be used and fitted in concealed areas where there's a risk of a fire.

6 Old camper vans have lots of fire risks, especially where the wiring is old and has been modified and repaired several times. The safest precaution in this situation is to fit a battery cut-off switch. This can be bought from motorsport specialists for less than £10 and requires an additional battery cable.

7 Incorporate fuses and cut-off switches for the electrical equipment that is operated within the camper van. A simple RCD plug/socket can be fitted between the mains hook up and the camper van's electrics, for instance. This will cut off the electricity if any problems arise, instead of blowing fuses or burning out appliances.

8 If a fire does occur, you need to have an exit plan to make sure everyone can get out of the camper van safely. This may seem obvious, but if doors are locked or cannot be opened from the inside, then it's not so easy to escape. Try getting out of the camper van blindfolded to recreate a smoke-filled interior.

9 If you find that particular areas of the camper van are difficult to get out of in the event of a fire, a life hammer could be the answer. This is used to shatter glass and will help with escaping from the camper van if a fire starts.

10 Aside from the risk of flames from a fire, another major problem is carbon monoxide poisoning, which is generated by gas cookers. Fit a portable CO meter inside the camper van to make sure you are alerted if there is such a risk.

An RCD can protect your electrics from blown fuses, burnt wiring and potential fires.

Make sure exit doors can be opened from the inside, such as the tailgate, rear doors and sliding door.

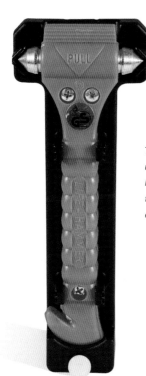

This life hammer can be used to smash glass and help you escape from the camper van in the event of a fire.

A battery-operated CO meter can alert you to an unknown fire or source where carbon monoxide levels are becoming dangerous.

FIRE STARTERS

Fire is one of the biggest disasters for a camper van and a major issue with a vehicle that may be carrying a wide variety of flammable products, such as gas bottles, petrol, cooking oil and lots of soft furnishings. Mix this with a variety of equipment that operates from 12-volt batteries and mains supplied electricity, and you can see that a fire has all the necessary ingredients to set alight and keep going.

It's worthwhile knowing the main causes of fires in order to be able to reduce the risk of one starting in the first place. The main causes are listed below with details on how to check them and help prevent the risk of a fire.

1 Dodgy wires: Any wiring that is frayed and exposed should be changed, repaired or covered. Previous owners may have modified the wiring or fitted additional electrical components, so check all wiring is safe and secure. Poor wiring can cause shorts and sparks, setting fire to upholstery.

2 What's that switch for? If you are unsure what a switch is for and cannot find out what it operates, it may be worthwhile investigating further. Trace any wiring from it and use a multimeter to see if it draws any current when it's switched on or off.

3 Live or dead: Some electrical components that are powered by the camper van's battery may be live all the time or only live when the ignition is on. Find out which components are always live and whether they pose a fire risk. If you are planning to fit additional components, decide whether it's safe to have them always live.

4 Overheating: Equipment such as a heater, inverter, fridge or stereo-amplifier should have built in cut-offs if they overheat. This is essential to help prevent them catching fire. Check these safety measures are incorporated and add your own fuses and cut-outs, if required.

5 Incorrectly connected equipment: Equipment inside the camper van must be correctly connected,

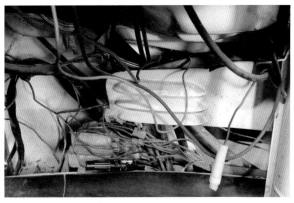

Chopped wires and dodgy connections can short out and cause fires.

Do you know what all the switches on the dashboard are for? Trace the wires for any you are unsure of.

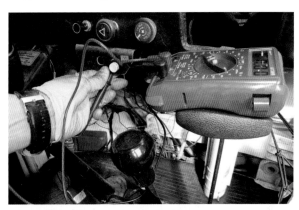

ABOVE LEFT: Use a multimeter to check for wires that are constantly live.

ABOVE RIGHT: The back of this fridge generates heat, so the vent above it helps to extract that heat and reduce the risk of it overheating.

LEFT: Make sure you know how to connect electrical equipment. This inverter, for instance, should be fitted with an earth spike.

especially devices such as an inverter or heater. If they are fitted wrongly, wires can burn out and cause fires.

6 Gas appliances: Cookers, fridges and heaters that are powered by gas must be correctly fitted to avoid leaks and explosions. If you are at all unsure, ask a qualified gas-fitter to complete the work for you.

7 Petrol pipes: This is the biggest cause of fires on older camper vans. Old petrol pipes, especially rubber pipes, perish and leak, resulting in engine bay fires. Renew all pipework if you are unsure of its age.

8 Rust protection: Wax-based products used in rust protection are flammable and can set on fire, especially during welding and grinding

repairs to the bodywork. If such repair work needs to be done, have a fire-extinguisher at the ready.

9 Flammable materials: Whilst camper van fires can be started by a number of causes, fire also needs the right materials. Upholstery, insulation, door cards and bottles of cooking oil are some of the ingredients that help keep a fire alive.

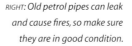

LEFT: Gas appliances must be correctly fitted and the gas bottles stored safely with adequate ventilation.

RIGHT: Old petrol pipes can leak and cause fires, so make sure they are in good condition.

LEFT: If your camper van is rust protected with wax and underseal, be cautious if any welding or grinding is required, as this protection is usually flammable.

RIGHT: Polystyrene insulation emits toxic fumes when on fire, so consider whether you want it installed in your camper van.

PROACTIVE PRECAUTIONS

It helps to be proactive with your camper van's interior to help reduce the risk of fire. When it comes to electrics, for instance, make sure you know what every wire is for and where it is routed (add labels, if necessary). Isolate electrical components when they are not in use, especially those that operate using mains-supplied electricity. This can be done on a simple level with extension leads that can be unplugged. Test components to make sure they are not faulty. This can involve a regular test of the fridge to make sure it becomes cold inside and doesn't overheat. Use a socket tester to check the wiring is correct and functioning properly in all electrical sockets.

Label wires to ensure you know what they are for in the future.

A socket tester can check whether an electrical socket is correctly wired and working properly.

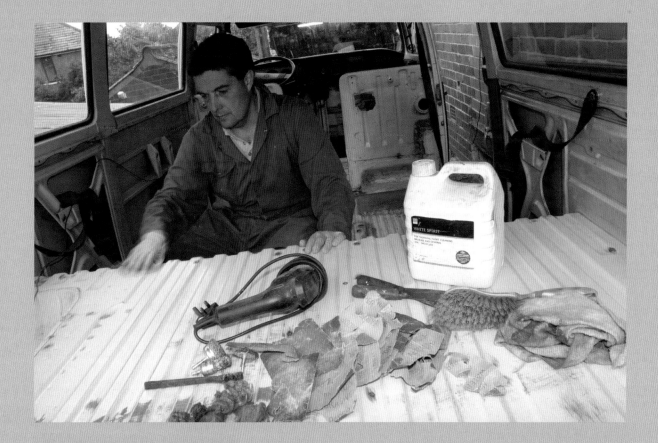

interior preparation

Preparing the interior of a camper van to fit an interior is just as important as fitting it. Insulation, soundproofing, rust protection, flooring and panelling all need to be considered and correctly fitted to ensure the interior is warm in winter, cool in summer and protected from the weather.

INSULATE AN INTERIOR

Heat needs to be kept in and out of a camper van, depending on the climate and the weather. There are a number of materials that can be used to line the walls and roof of a camper van to help keep it warm when it's cold outside and cool when the sun is beating down on the roof.

Heat-reflective material can be used to protect the camper van from warming up too much in the sun. This can be bought in a roll, cut to size and fixed to the inside walls of the camper van using spray adhesive. It can also act as insulation for keeping heat inside the camper van, helping to prevent it escaping through the walls.

Specialists such as Just Kampers produce an insulation and panelling kit for specific vans such as the VW T4. This not only includes insulation material, but also the plastic panels that can transform a van into a camper van.

Other forms of insulation include polystyrene, which is cheap to buy, easy to cut and lightweight. It can be bought in large blocks and cut with a knife. Use a small amount of adhesive to fix it in position behind panels. The disadvantage with polystyrene is that it cannot be compressed, so if it's too thick to fit

Heat-reflective material can be fitted to the inside walls of the camper van to help keep heat in and out.

This insulation kit from Just Kampers includes the panelling to line the inside of a Volkswagen T4 van.

Polystyrene can be cut into blocks and slotted behind panels inside a camper van.

behind a panel, it may be feasible to trim it, but it could be simpler to source another block. Another problem with polystyrene and many other forms of insulation is that it is flammable and highly toxic when it is on fire. If you intend to use as many non-flammable materials as possible in your camper van, look for another type of insulation to polystyrene.

Similarly, cheap insulation is carpet underlay, which is easy to cut to shape using a knife. However, it is heavy and more suitable for insulating floors instead of walls.

Fitting soft, loft insulation-style material is a popular method for keeping a camper van warm. Rockwool is a popular material, which is cheap to buy and effective at keeping heat inside a camper van. The disadvantage with it is that it is very good at absorbing moisture, so it may soak up condensation and any water that leaks into the camper van. Some people choose to fit this type of insulation inside plastic sheeting or bags to help reduce the risk of moisture absorption. However, any areas of the camper van that do not trap water are usually safe to insulate

without the need to use plastic sheeting or bags. The following steps outline some points you need to consider when using this type of insulation.

1 If the area you intend to insulate has some means of retaining the insulation, such as strengthening beams and channels, then the insulation can be cut to size and wedged into position without having to glue it down.

2 Where a panel has no means of holding the insulation in position, use a spray adhesive. This will make

Here the insulation can be wedged and held in position with surrounding strengthening beams and panelling.

Spray-on adhesive can be used to secure insulation to a panel that offers no means of holding it.

Doors without wind-down windows can be filled with insulation, but make sure the locking and opening mechanisms can still be operated.

Conceal insulation with panelling for a neater finish, but make sure you can check it periodically for moisture absorption.

it more difficult to remove the insulation, but at least it will stay in position and do its job of keeping heat inside the camper van.

3   If you are insulating a rear door, the material can be squashed inside it without having to glue it. Make sure it doesn't obstruct any moving parts, such as the door lock and handle mechanism.

4   Always fit trim panels over insulation – never leave it exposed. Make sure the panels can be removed to check for moisture. An insulated panel is also a favourite home for mice, so if your camper van is laid up for the winter, you may want to check it over before using it again.

REDUCING RATTLES, DRAUGHTS AND NOISE

When you are driving along in your camper van, you may discover there are whistling sounds from around the doors or windscreen, where air is leaking through the seals. This can become more of a problem when it rains and water starts to leak into the camper van. The best solution here is to renew the seals and, in most cases, the work involved isn't particularly complicated, but can be awkward and frustrating. This section provides several general steps to show what's usually involved in fitting new seals, but you may find it's a little different on your own camper van.

Seals around doors are much easier to renew and often involve cutting or tearing off the old stuff, before fitting a new seal into position. New rubber seals around doors often mean the door is initially harder to close, but the lack of draughts and whistles is worth the extra effort required to slam the door shut.

It also helps to renew the seals and trim for wind-down windows and quarterlights to keep leaks and draughts away. Rebuild kits are available for a number of vehicles, although the work involved can be complicated, so look for fitting guides before you spend your money.

Road noise and vibrations can also become annoying, especially when driving, but many of these problems can be reduced or eradicated with sound-deadening material to help cut out noise and stop panels rattling.

HOW TO RENEW RUBBER SEALS FOR WINDOWS AND WINDSCREENS

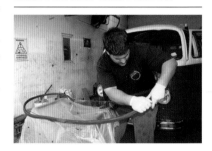

The work involved in removing old rubber seals around windows and windscreens and fitting new seals varies between different camper vans, so the following steps provide a general overview of what's usually involved. The photographs show the window and windscreen seals being renewed on a VW Bay Window camper van.

ABOVE LEFT AND RIGHT: *Renewing rubber seals around the doors is quite straightforward and often effective for stopping leaks and draughts.*

Renewing the seals and parts for door glass helps to ensure an airtight seal.

Quarterlights can whistle and leak, but are often quite complicated to overhaul.

Renewing Rubber Seals

1 The seals for fixed glass often need to be partly cut out to help remove the glass and renew all of the seal. Carefully cut around the seal, but make sure you are ready to catch the glass, just in case it falls out.

2 Ask someone to help you remove the glass by pushing from the inside whilst you stand on the outside, ready and waiting to catch the glass. Wear gloves to protect your hands from the sharp edges of the glass.

3 Clean the glass and around where the glass is fitted on the camper van. Trial fit the new seal to make sure it is the correct size.

4 Fit a length of wire around the seal. This will be removed after the glass has been fitted and will be pulled out from inside to help locate the seal.

5 Apply a smear of washing-up liquid around the edge of the metal where the glass and seal will be fitted. This lubrication will help to manoeuvre the glass and seal into position.

6 Fit the glass in position, making sure the seal locates correctly and the ends of the wire that is wrapped around its outer edge are inside the camper van.

7 Many windscreen specialists use suction tools to help locate and hold the glass when fitting it. If you can borrow a set or decide to buy them, then they can make fitting glass a lot easier and safer.

TOOLBOX

- Length of wire
- Screwdrivers
- Washing-up liquid

Difficulty level: 4/5
On your own? No
Time: From 1 hour

Use a knife to cut around the edges of the old seal to remove it.

Peel off the old seal after cutting around it, making sure the glass doesn't fall out.

Ask someone to push the glass from inside whilst you stand outside and remove it.

Trial fit the new seal to make sure it fits.

Fit a length of wire around the new seal to help fit it onto the camper van.

8   Push down hard around the edges of the glass to help force it into position, then start to remove the wire from around the edge of the seal. Push the glass into position where the wire is being extracted. This requires at least two people.

9   Make sure the edges of the seal fit over the outside and inside of the bodywork on the camper van. Carefully use a screwdriver to work the edges of the rubber seal into position.

Washing-up liquid is a useful lubricant for fitting the glass back into position.

Carefully fit the glass in position, making sure the ends of the wire are inside the camper van.

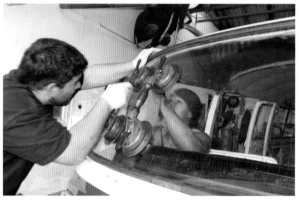

Professionals often use suction tools to help fit glass.

Push hard around the edges of the glass and pull the wire out to locate the seal.

Carefully lever around the edges of the seal to make sure it is correctly seated.

SOUND-DEADENING

Sound-deadening involves reducing the risk of panel vibration, which amplifies road and engine noise. However, it can also be used to reduce distortion and help some sounds, such as the noise from speakers, which needs to be as clear as possible.

Noise Reduction

1   Remove any trim from inside the wheel arches, scrape off any dirt, then spray a couple of coats of underseal onto the metalwork. This will help to sound deaden the panels from road noise and vibrations.

2   Carpet underlay is a useful and cheap sound-deadening material. It can be cut with a knife and fitted

Scrape off as much dirt as possible from inside the wheel arches.

Spray underseal onto the clean metal of the wheel arches to help reduce road noise and vibrations.

underneath flooring or secured to panels with adhesive or simple mounting brackets and grub screws.

Carpet underlay is a cheap source of sound-deadening material and insulation.

Carpet underlay can be secured to a panel with a homemade mounting bracket and screws.

3 Sound-deadening material can be purchased from car audio specialists. In most cases, you won't need to line a panel in this material, just fit a small square to reduce panel vibration.

Professional sound-deadening material is available from car audio specialists. Most of it can be cut with scissors or a knife.

Sound-deadening material doesn't need to cover an entire panel to prevent it vibrating.

Sound-Deadening for Sound

Sound-deadening isn't solely used to keep noise to a minimum. It's also useful for improving the sound quality from any speakers fitted inside the camper van. The speakers create a lot of noise and, consequently, this noise can result in panel vibration, especially around the bodywork where the speakers are fitted. The solution is to fit sound-deadening material around where each speaker is fitted to help reduce the risk of panel vibration. The following steps show how this can be achieved.

1 Remove the speaker from its location and detach its wiring at the back. Most speakers are secured with a series of screws around the edges. If the speaker is mounted in a pod, it may be easier to remove this with the speaker first.

Most speakers are secured with a series of screws.

Detach the wiring from the back of the speaker, noting how the wires are fitted.

Strips of sound-deadening material can be fitted behind a speaker to further reduce vibrations.

2 Fit strips of sound-deadening material to the panelwork that is behind the speaker. This will help to reduce vibrations caused by noise that comes out of the rear of the speaker.

Most sound-deadening material can be cut with scissors or a knife.

3 Cut a piece of sound-deadening material that's larger than the hole where the speaker is fitted. Most sound-deadening material has an adhesive backing, so stick it over the hole, then cut it out, leaving sufficient material in place.

Cut out a piece of sound-deadening material, fit it over the speaker hole then cut around the hole to be able to refit the speaker.

Refit the speaker, connecting the wires to their respective terminals.

4 Refit the speaker using its original mounting screws, then carefully apply a bead of silicone sealant around the edges of the speaker. This will help to further absorb any vibrations from the speaker.

You may need to cut the sound-deadening material to find the locating holes for the screws.

Apply a bead of silicone sealant to further seal the speaker from unwanted panel vibration.

HEADLINING

The underside of the roof area of a camper van needs to be lined in some type of material to prevent moisture settling and dripping down. This is particularly important if the roof is made of metal.

There are a number of ways of lining the inside of a roof. The following section outlines some of the popular solutions and how they can be fitted.

◆ Bows and vinyl: The traditional car manufacturer's approach to headlining, consisting of bows that stretch across the roof and a vinyl covering with space between it and the roof, so there's less chance of hurting your head.
◆ Carpet: Gluing, screwing and riveting carpet to the underside of the roof is easier than using bows and vinyl. It can be trimmed *in situ* and, providing you're skilled at carpet trimming, it's easy to achieve a professional finish. However, this solution is not suitable if the underside of the roof is not smooth or consists of several strengthening beams.

◆ Hardboard covers: Modern panel vans may have hardboard panels lining the underside of the roof. These can be removed, trimmed and refitted, if required.
◆ Flexible plywood: Strengthening beams on the underside of a roof can be concealed with sheets of flexible plywood, which in turn can be covered in fabric or painted. The plywood can be secured to the strengthening beams with screws.

HOW TO FIT A FLOOR

The floor of the living area inside a camper van can be left as bare metal, but it looks so much better if it is covered. There are a variety of materials that can be used. Popular choices include vinyl, wood laminate and carpet. There are advantages and disadvantages with all of these options. A laminated floor looks effective but adds weight to the vehicle, unless you use a wood laminate effect vinyl. Carpet can get wet and become difficult to keep clean and dry. Vinyl can get torn or scratched (as can a laminated floor).

Traditional vinyl covering is secured with a bowed framework, so it's not directly attached to the underside of the roof.

Fitting carpet directly on to the underside of the roof is one of the easiest and most cost effective approaches.

Hardboard panels are fitted as standard to the underside of many modern vans.

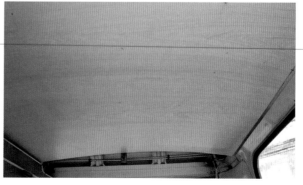

Flexible plywood can cover the underside of a roof that has strengthening beams, resulting in a smooth finish.

An uneven floor needs a flat covering before vinyl or carpet can be fitted over it.

Laminated floors are popular in homes and also in camper vans, but are heavier than carpets or vinyl.

The front floor is higher than the rear in this van, but after fitting a raised floor in the rear, everything is at the same level.

This shallow pine framework is sufficient to allow a flat false floor to be fitted to cover the van's original ribbed floor.

Most van floors are ribbed to add extra rigidity to them and stop them flexing and warping when heavy loads are placed on top of them. Consequently, when flooring such as carpet or vinyl is laid over such a surface, the unevenness of the floor is noticeable, even if you fit thick underlay. The solution to such a problem is to lay hardboard or plywood first to create a flat surface.

Some vans have wheel arches that protrude inside the van, which can limit space. One solution, which is only really applicable to vans with a high roof, is to raise the floor with wood before laying a new floor on top. This is also a useful solution for a van where the floor at the front (around the driver and passenger seats) is higher than the floor in the rear – raising the rear floor results in all the floor area inside the van being at the same level.

The following steps show how to fit vinyl flooring, which is similar to fitting carpet. The preparation work can take longer than cutting out the carpet or vinyl and fitting it, so set aside a long weekend to complete all of the work involved and allow time for further jobs.

Raising a Floor

If the height of the floor in a van is different to the height of the floor in the cabin, then you may want to consider raising the height of the floor in the rear to ensure all of the floor area is at the same height. The best way to raise a floor is to build a wooden framework. Use lightweight wood such as pine and create a box-sectional structure that is secured together with screws. It's worthwhile fixing this wood to the floor of the van to reduce the risk of unwanted rattles and movement in the new floor.

Use plywood for the new floor and secure it to the wooden framework underneath – consider insulating

---

TOOLBOX

- Paint brush
- Scraper
- Sharp knife for cutting vinyl/carpet
- Steel-wire brushes
- Tape-measure
- Wet and dry paper (various grades)
- White spirit

Difficulty level: 2/5
On your own? Yes
Time: from 3 hours

Remove as much as possible from the interior of the van before fitting the flooring.

Give the floor a thorough scrape and scrub.

Brush and vacuum from the top down to remove as much dirt as possible.

If you spot rust or unwanted holes, fix them before fitting the flooring.

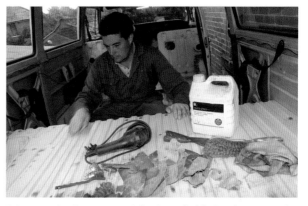

Paint protecting the camper van's floor is worthwhile. Start by prepping the surfaces with wet and dry paper.

White gloss paint for metal surfaces produces a clean finish.

Hard-wearing red oxide and similar paints can be used for floor areas.

Vinyl or carpet will feel uneven on ribbed floors, so lay a sheet of hardboard or plywood down first.

under the new floor and routing electrical cables.

Calculating how much extra height you need can be difficult. Take into account the height of the wooden framework and the thickness of the plywood to make sure the new floor is at the same level as the floor in the cabin.

If you need to fit seats or other heavy objects on top of the new floor, do not mount them solely to the plywood and framework. Instead, locate any fixing points on the van's original steel floor and make sure these are used. This is especially important for seats and seatbelt fixing points, but equally important for a fridge or cupboard that could rip through any mounting points in the raised wooden floor in the event of an accident.

1   Remove as much of the interior as possible, to be able to fit the flooring. Items such as seating and a kitchen can sit on top of the flooring, which saves on having to cut the material around them.

2   Once you have a bare floor, inspect it closely for corrosion. Scrape off any dirt and use a brush and vacuum cleaner to remove it. Any dirt that isn't removed will become trapped under the flooring.

3   If you find any corrosion in the floor, don't ignore it. Rust and holes will not cure themselves by covering over them with flooring. Cut out the rot and have new metal welded in position.

4   Unless the floor is in pristine condition, it may be worthwhile painting to protect it from corrosion. Start

by sanding down the floor with 80 grit wet and dry paper. Brush away the debris and wipe down the floor with panel wipe or white spirit.

5   Apply a couple of coats of suitable metal paint (make sure the floor is clear of dirt) to the floor, allowing sufficient time for the paint to dry between each coat.

6   If the floor is ribbed (i.e. not perfectly flat), then this unevenness won't be sufficiently covered with a layer of vinyl or carpet. Instead, you will need to fit something flat, such as hardboard, plywood or rubber matting. This can be fitted in sections.

7   If rubber matting is laid down on the floor, this can be used as a template in which to cut out the new carpet or vinyl. Lay it down on top of the new flooring and cut around

it. If you don't have this, measure the floor area and cut it out.

8 Fit the vinyl or carpet into position, making sure it lines up with any exposed sides, such as along the sliding door. Vinyl is easy to trim in situ with a pair of scissors, so if you need to cut off some excess after it has been fitted, you won't need to remove it from the van.

9 After fitting the carpet or vinyl, you may find some mounting or drainage holes are covered over, so locate these and cut holes in the new flooring to make sure they can be used again.

10 Make sure anything that's mounted to the floor (table, seating) can be fitted before deciding whether you need to glue the carpet or vinyl to the floor. Once a kitchen has been installed, you may find this isn't necessary and so the flooring will be easier to remove in the future.

If you have an existing rubber mat or covering for the floor, use it as a template to cut out the new floor.

Fit the carpet or vinyl into the van, making sure it lines up with any exposed sides, such as next to the sliding door.

Vinyl can be trimmed with a pair of scissors, so if there is any excess, it can be removed after the vinyl has been fitted.

Find the mounting points for seats, tables and other fixings, then cut them out of the new flooring.

The tripod table mount in the middle of the floor is bolted in position and also helps to prevent the vinyl from moving.

You may find that once the entire interior has been fitted, you won't need to glue the carpet or vinyl down.

Carpet looks effective and provides a warm feel to an interior, but is difficult to keep clean and dry.

This carpet has piping along its edges, helping to reduce the risk of it fraying. It can also be removed from the van and cleaned.

Carpeting

The steps that show how to fit vinyl flooring can also be applied to fitting carpet. Carpet can look cosier, but it's more difficult to keep clean and dry than vinyl that can be brushed and wiped over with a cloth. If you intend to remove the carpet and clean it, the edges will become frayed, so consider having some piping fitted.

Carpet can certainly be a cheap solution, especially if you have a spare piece leftover from your home. However, it will need a sharp knife to cut through it and can look tatty at the edges if you don't make a clean cut.

HOW TO COVER A PANEL WITH HARDBOARD

Materials including hardboard and plywood are ideal for making your own panels or covering existing panels that may be damaged, tatty or full of holes. The following steps show what's involved in covering an old seatboard (the board below a rock-and-roll bed), which in this case, has multiple holes for an assortment of speakers. However, the instructions can also help with making your own panels to fit inside a camper van.

TOOLBOX

- Bolts and screws
- Electric drill with 4–8mm drill bits
- Jigsaw with wood cutting blade
- Pencil
- Scraper
- Sharp knife

Difficulty level: 2/5
On your own? Yes
Time: 1 hour

1　Remove any objects from the panel that will prevent the hardboard fitting flush to it. The seatboard shown here has lots of holes in it for old speakers and some tatty vinyl, which can be removed with a scraper.

2　Take a new or clean piece of hardboard and lay the old panel onto the underside of it. Mark around the old panel and onto the underside of the hardboard to see where you need to cut.

3　A jigsaw is the quickest method of cutting through hardboard. Set the jigsaw to a slow speed and take your time to avoid a rough finish. If you don't have a jigsaw, hardboard can be cut with a sharp knife.

4　After cutting out the hardboard, check it fully covers the old panel by laying it on top. If the hardboard is too small, you may be able to use it and add an extra bit, then cover it all in vinyl.

5　If any objects need to protrude through the panel, cut out the relevant sections in the new hardboard cover using a sharp knife (e.g. a Stanley knife). This can be awkward to measure.

6　Clamp the hardboard onto the seatboard. You're now ready to mount the hardboard in position with screws, but first see the next step for any additional mounts that may need to be fitted.

7　Some seatboards are mounted to the rock-and-roll bed with brackets and bolts. If this is the case, slowly drill through these mounting points in the back of the old seatboard and through to the new

If you are covering an old panel, remove as much unwanted material off the front of it as possible.

Use the old panel as a template to mark out the shape of the new covering.

Hardboard can be cut with a jigsaw. Set the tool to its slowest speed and take your time.

Check the new panel fully covers the old one.

This lock for a rock-and-roll bed must not be covered by the new hardboard, so measure around it and cut out its shape.

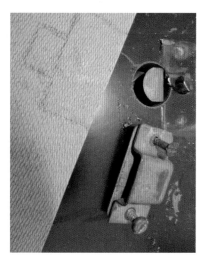

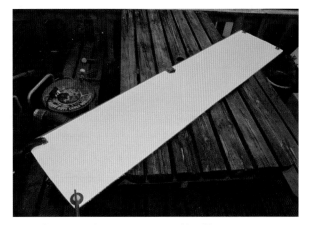

Clamp the new panel into position on top of the old one.

Drill pilot holes for any mounting bolts through from the back of the old seatboard.

After drilling a pilot hole, drill a larger hole from the front to reduce the risk of damaging the face of the hardboard.

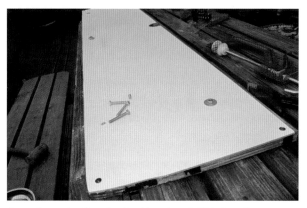

Secure the new hardboard to the old seatboard with bolts and screws.

hardboard. Use a small 4mm drill bit to make a pilot hole.

8 Drilling through the back of the hardboard will splinter and blister it, so after drilling the small holes in the last step, finish off with larger holes on the front of the hardboard using a drill bit that's large enough to fit the mounting bolts through.

9 Secure the mounting brackets with suitable bolts. You may also want to secure the edges of the hardboard to the seatboard using small wood screws. You won't need to drill any holes to fit wood screws.

TOOLBOX

· Masking or gaffer tape
· Pencil
· Scissors
· Sharp knife
· Staple gun

Difficulty level: 1/5
On your own? Yes
Time: 1 hour

1 Remove the panel from the camper van, clean any dirt from it and check its condition. If a hardboard panel is cracked, for example, it can often be repaired with gaffer tape or masking tape.

2 If a panel is beyond rescuing, it may be easier to cut out a new one from a sheet of hardboard. Use the old one as a template and mark round it on the new panel, then cut it out with a sharp knife.

HOW TO UPHOLSTER A PANEL

The panels inside a camper van can be covered in material to transform their appearance. The following steps outline a straightforward DIY approach to fitting material over an existing panel. The fabric shown in the photographs was bought at a market and the tools and other materials used are all readily available.

Some panels are secured with screws, whereas this panel at the front of a VW Bay Window is wedged into position.

If the panel is broken, it may be possible to hold it together with gaffer tape, which will be hidden by the new material.

If you need to make a new panel, use the old one as a template.

Curved edges are difficult to cut out, so use the old panel as a guide when cutting.

3 Lay the front of the panel onto the underside of the fabric you want to cover it in. Cut the fabric leaving 50–75mm spare around the perimeter. This will be used to wrap around the edges and secure to the back of the panel.

4 Fold the fabric over and onto the back of the panel, securing it with masking tape. You may need to cut the fabric to help fold it over and avoid creases on the exposed side of the panel.

5 Trim any excess fabric at the corners where it is folded over several times, but make sure there's sufficient fabric remaining to be able to secure it to the back of the panel.

6 If there are any holes in the panel, cut a slot in the centre of the fabric, then cut towards the edges of the hole. Cut the fabric into several sections, then secure it to the back of the panel with masking tape.

7 When you've finished securing the fabric to the back of the panel, turn it over and check for creases. Move your hand over the surface of the fabric to look see where it sags. You

may need to lift the masking tape and refit it in places.

8 The fabric needs to be secured to the back of the panel with something better than masking tape. Spray adhesive can be used to hold the fabric to the front of the panel. At the back, fit short staples using a staple gun.

9 When you've finished, refit the panel and secure it with whatever fixings were originally used. You may have to use a bradawl to locate any original screw holes in the panel.

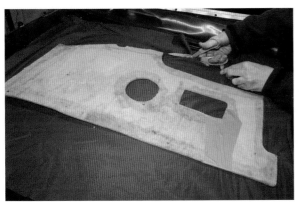

Cut the fabric, leaving 5–8cm spare around the perimeter of the panel.

Fold the fabric over and secure it to the underside of the panel.

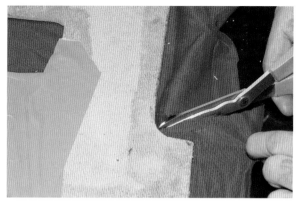

This curved edge will crease the fabric when it's folded over, so cut it first.

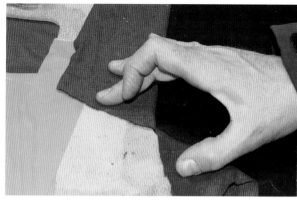

Cutting the fabric up to the edge of the panel helps to fold it over this curved section and eliminate creases.

Cut off any excess fabric at the corners. This will help to secure the corners to the back of the panel without having too much fabric.

Where there's a hole in the panel, the fabric will need to be cut into sections to be able to wrap it around the edges.

Use lots of masking tape to secure the sections of fabric that have been cut for the hole in the panel.

Turn the panel over to see the front of the fabric. Look for creases.

Staples can be used to secure the fabric to the back of the panel, but make sure they don't go all the way through the hardboard.

Refit the panel and secure it with any original fixings. This panel is wedged into position.

HOW TO VINYL WRAP A PANEL

One of the most effective methods of reviving an old panel or producing a stunning finish to a wide range of surfaces is to wrap it in vinyl. The vinyl-wrapping market is huge and there are a wide range of colours and designs available, ranging from solid reds and blues to carbon fibre effect finishes, stripes and spots.

The work involved in fitting vinyl is quite straightforward, but mistakes are easy to make. Ensure the surface you intend to wrap is clean. Any major imperfections won't be hidden by the vinyl.

Vinyl can be fitted dry or wet using water with baby shampoo or a special applicator. Wet fitting allows you to move the vinyl around, whereas dry fitting means you have to lift the vinyl if it's incorrectly positioned. The following steps show how to dry fit vinyl.

Typical problems that can arise when fitting vinyl include air bubbles. If you notice air bubbles when initially laying the vinyl, lift it up and refit it. If they are noticed later, then they can be removed by heating up the vinyl with a hair-dryer or heat gun and pricking each bubble – this is shown in the following steps. However, avoid overheating the vinyl; most vinyl can be safely heated to around 32˚C.

Vinyl can be fitted over objects that are not perfectly flat and this is covered in the next section in the chapter.

Popular vinyl manufacturers include 3M, Avery, Hexis, Metamark and APA. They make a variety of different types of vinyl, suitable for different applications. Many of their products offer bubble-free fitting.

If you want to vinyl wrap the side of a kitchen cupboard door or a seatboard, then a top-quality vinyl will ensure a good finish and a straightforward application, but a cheaper brand can also work. Cheap vinyl is less forgiving, so don't expect to be able to apply it and lift it off several times to remove unwanted air bubbles (it will quickly become stretched and distorted). The following steps show how to fit some cheap vinyl sourced on eBay that cost £4 for a 1.5m roll. This is ideal for flat surfaces, but would prove difficult to apply on uneven surfaces where a better quality vinyl could be stretched and shaped.

1   Make sure the vinyl you have for the panel you intend to cover is large enough. If the vinyl is not large enough, you may be able to fit it in sections, especially if the pattern on the vinyl can be lined up.

2   Make sure the surface is spotlessly clean. Any imperfections may not be hidden by the vinyl. Trim the vinyl to the shape of the panel you want to cover. Some vinyl can be wrapped around and over a panel, whereas thicker vinyl may lift, so will need trimming.

3   Place the vinyl over the panel, then start to peel off the backing paper and smooth the vinyl onto the panel. You can use your hands to smooth it down, but a felt-edged squeegee or similar tool is better.

4   If bubbles or creases start to appear in the vinyl, you will need to lift it off and re-apply it. This may stretch and distort the vinyl (more so with cheap vinyl), so carefully lift it up. If it becomes difficult to apply, you may need to throw it away and start again.

TOOLBOX

- Felt-edged squeegee or old credit card wrapped in a soft cloth
- Hair-dryer or heat-gun
- Knife
- Scissors
- Straight edge

Difficulty level: 2/5
On your own? Yes
Time: from 1 hour

VINYL TYPES

- Cast films – this is the preferred vinyl used by most wrapping specialists. It's made from a liquid, which is allowed to spread and form a thin layer. Cast films are stable (they don't react with other chemicals) and shrinkage is minimal. The thin material (usually around 60 microns) is easy to cut and apply over uneven surfaces.
- Polymeric calendered films – made from highly stabilized polymeric plastic that is passed through rollers during manufacture to progressively flatten it into a roll of film, taking its surface finish from the rollers. The added polymers reduce the risk of shrinkage and the resulting material is suitable for fitting on both flat and curved surfaces, but is not quite as compliant as cast films.
- Monomeric calendered films – the cheapest vinyl to manufacture. Liable to shrinkage, curling and peeling. Useful for short-term stickers and decals.

5   Once the vinyl has been fitted, look closely for air bubbles. Any air bubbles that are close to the outside perimeter of the vinyl can often be pushed out using your fingers.

6   Any air bubbles that are difficult to push out will need to be gently heated with a hair-dryer or heatgun, then pricked with a knife and smoothed over. Be careful not to burn your fingers.

ABOVE: This vinyl is being used to cover a kitchen worktop. It's not wide enough, but the pattern is easy to match, so an additional strip can be fitted.

TOP RIGHT: Trim the vinyl to the shape of the panel. Some vinyl can be wrapped around the back of a panel.

LEFT: The backing paper on some vinyl has squares on it, which helps to cut straight lines.

Progressively peel off the backing paper and smooth the vinyl onto the panel using your hands or a felt edged squeegee.

An extra pair of hands helps to smooth the vinyl down on to the panel. If bubbles or creases appear, lift the vinyl and refit it.

Some of these bubbles can be removed by pushing them out to the edge of the panel.

Any bubbles that cannot be forced out, will need to be gently heated up with a hair-dryer or heat gun. Don't melt the vinyl.

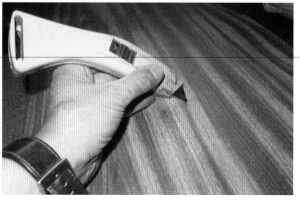

Once a bubble has been warmed up, prick it with a knife and push it down with a cloth to remove the air and flatten the vinyl.

HOW TO VINYL WRAP AN UNEVEN OBJECT

Uneven objects are harder to vinyl wrap than a flat panel. The vinyl needs to be warmed, stretched and shaped around the object. A good-quality vinyl is better, but you may want to practice with some cheap vinyl first.

Objects ranging from instrument housings to table legs can all be wrapped in vinyl. The following steps show how to wrap a curved plastic cover and an object with a hole in the middle (e.g. an instrument pod or surround for a clock).

TOOLBOX

- Craft knife
- Felt-edged squeegee or old credit card wrapped in a soft cloth
- Gloves
- Hair-dryer or heat-gun

Difficulty level: 2/5
On your own? Possible
Time: from 1 hour

1 Remove the panel or object to be wrapped and thoroughly clean it with methylated spirit. Use cotton-buds to clean in grooves and around edges. Any imperfections may not be hidden by the vinyl.

2 Measure and cut a suitable size of vinyl. With an extra person, heat the vinyl with a heat gun or hair-dryer, then lay it over the panel. Don't overheat the vinyl. It should be warmed to no more than 32°C. If it gets too hot, it will melt or burn.

3 Mould the vinyl over the panel, then apply some more heat with the heat gun (avoid burning your hands). Make sure no air gets trapped under the vinyl and it doesn't get creased. Smooth the vinyl onto the panel by hand.

4 If nobody is available to help, try standing the heat-gun so the nozzle is pointing upwards (make sure

Thoroughly clean the object to be wrapped. Any dirt won't help the vinyl to stick to the object.

Cut a piece of vinyl to cover the object and heat it up with a hair-dryer or heat gun before fitting it.

Keep heating the vinyl as you lift and mould it over the object.

Standing a heat gun facing upwards enables you to warm the vinyl on your own.

Use a felt-edged squeegee to push the vinyl into any grooves in the object.

Trim off any excess vinyl using a craft knife.

Gently warm the vinyl again to help mould it around the object.

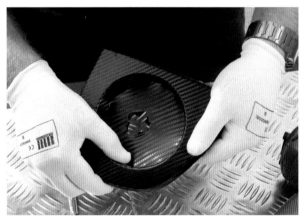

An object with a hole in the middle can be wrapped. After fitting the vinyl, cut a hole through it and warm up the vinyl to begin moulding it.

Wrap the vinyl around the edges of the hole. Extra pieces of vinyl may need to be fitted to cover everything inside the hole.

it's secure). Leave it switched on and move the panel above it to warm the vinyl. The vinyl has to be moulded to the panel, so it needs to be warmed up.

5 Use a felt-edged squeegee to push the vinyl into any grooves or mould it around any ridges or edges. Don't push too hard as the squeegee can cut through the vinyl. Vinyl stockists usually sell felt-edged squeegees.

6 When you're satisfied the panel has been covered in vinyl, trim off any excess with a craft knife (available from craft shops such as Hobby Craft). Use your fingers as a guide when trimming, but don't get them in the way of the sharp blade.

7 Gently heat the vinyl once more to help change its shape and mould it to the panel. If any air bubbles are found, see step 6 in the previous guide to fitting vinyl onto a flat panel to find out how to remove them.

8 Panels such as a light or instrument surround are difficult to cover, but possible. Fit the vinyl over the hole in the surround, then cut a small hole in the middle, heat it up and carefully push it through.

9 When the hole is large enough to wrap around the inner edges of the surround, warm it up and carefully smooth down before trimming off the excess. If the inner edges are not fully covered, a small patch of vinyl can be fitted.

HOW TO FIT CURTAINS

If you want to sleep inside your camper van, then curtains or blinds are essential. A set of curtains can be relatively simple to make, using Velcro to attach pieces of material around each window. However, for a more professional look, use a length of curtain wire, cut a piece of material to twice the required size, sew it in half and along the edges for a neat finish and feed the curtain wire through. The following steps go a stage further and show how the top edge of a curtain can be sewn to make a small loop inside it, which can be used to feed the curtain wire through.

Curtain wire can be found at DIY stores, eBay, Amazon and local markets. It can be cut to size and the end fixings (loops or hooks) screwed in position. The wire is best secured inside the van using grub screws.

Making and fitting curtains can be as quick or as time-consuming as you want. If you want a good finish, don't rush and if you've never sewed before, be prepared to learn or find someone who can.

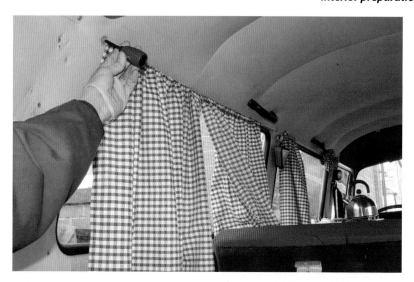

These curtains are fitted to a Wellhouse Leisure converted Toyota Hiace and include one that stretches behind the front cab.

TOOLBOX

- 3–4mm drill bit
- Electric drill
- Marker pen
- Material for curtains
- Scissors for cutting material
- Screwdriver
- Sewing kit or sewing machine
- Tape-measure

Difficulty level: 2/5
On your own? Yes
Time: 2+ hours

Measure the length of the curtain wire, which must be longer than the width of the window.

Cut a length of curtain wire and fit loops or hooks at the ends.

From the outside of the camper van, measure the width of the glass.

The curtain needs to be taller than the height of the window.

Each curtain should cover at least two-thirds of the width of the window.

The edge of the curtain in the lower part of this photograph is the top of the curtain where the curtain wire will be fed through.

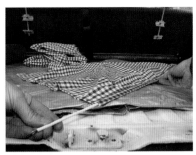

Feed the curtain wire through the top loop in the curtain.

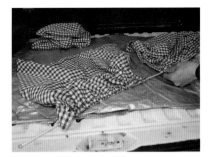

Make a second curtain and feed the curtain wire through.

Trial fit the curtain and mark the position of the ends of the curtain wire.

Carefully drill a pilot hole to mount the curtain wire.

Secure both ends of the curtain wire to the inside of the camper van with grub screws.

1 Measure the required length of the curtain wire. It will be fitted above the window so should be longer than the width of the glass.
2 Cut the curtain wire to length and fit hooks or loops at the ends, which will be used to fix the ends of the wire to the inside of the camper van.
3 Measure the width of the glass that will be covered by the curtain – do this from the outside of the camper van, as it's easier.
4 Measure the height of the glass and the distance from roughly where the curtain wire will be fitted to 3–5cm below the window.
5 Using the measurements from the last steps, cut a piece of material that's two-thirds the length of the curtain wire and 3–5cm longer than the distance from the curtain wire to below the window. This will form one of two curtains.
6 Fold over and sew the edges of the material to make a hem. Along the top edge, don't sew it so tight, but make sure there's a sufficient gap to feed the curtain wire through.
7 Take the curtain you've made and feed the curtain wire through the top loop that has been sewn into it. Make sure the curtain moves freely along the wire.

Make sure the curtains for adjacent windows are similar in length.

8 Make a second curtain to the same dimensions as the first one, then feed the curtain wire through its top edge. Check that both curtains can move freely.
9 Trial fit the curtain wire in position and mark the location of the hooks/loops at each end, making sure the curtain covers the entire window.
10 Most camper van walls are double-skinned along the edges, so care- fully drill a 3–4mm pilot hole in the two marks made in the last step.
11 Use grub screws to secure the ends of the curtain wire to the holes drilled in the last step. Make sure the hooks/loops on the ends of the curtain wire don't slip over the head of the grub screws.
12 Continue making curtains for all the other windows. Stick to simi- lar lengths, especially for adjacent windows.

HOW TO REMOVE A SPARE WHEEL WELL

A spare wheel in the rear of a van isn't the best use of interior space, particularly if you want to sleep in the back. Of course, the easiest solution is to simply remove the spare wheel and put some padding over the hole. However, the space underneath the spare wheel well is wasted and can be used for storage or the location of a leisure battery.

Most spare wheel wells consist of a curved panel that's secured to the van with spot welds. These can be removed by drilling through the spot welds, which is outlined in the following steps. However, you may also need to cut around the well with a hacksaw and lever it out by bending the edges of it.

Make sure you wear goggles, gloves and other protective clothing when drilling or cutting the metalwork. The cut metal will be sharp, so wear gardening gloves or something similar.

Once the spare wheel well has been removed, new panelwork may need to be cut to size and fitted, especially in a rear-engined camper van, where engine or petrol fumes need to be isolated. Then, additional upholstery can be made to cover the hole and expand the bed for instance. The following steps show how to do all of this type of work. Before starting, look underneath the spare wheel well to make sure you are not going to damage anything when drilling and removing this panel.

1   Look around the edges of the spare wheel well for a series of indentations. These are usually spot welds and can be drilled out. First, mark them with a centre punch to help drill through them.
2   Drill through the spot welds using a suitable sized drill bit (e.g. 10mm). You may want to start with a small drill bit first. Don't drill all the way through, just through the first layer of metal.
3   After drilling several of the spot welds, you may wonder why the spare wheel well isn't popping up. Use a hammer and chisel to help separate it. This will also help to see if you've missed any of the spot welds.
4   Some areas of the spare wheel well may be difficult to access with a drill or may need to be cut out. If

you have an angle grinder with a cutting disc, or a jigsaw, this will be quick to complete, but check what's underneath the spare wheel well. A hacksaw can also be used.
5   Once you have cut all the way round the spare wheel well, it can be removed. Watch your fingers on the sharp metal edges when removing it. If any wires run through the spare wheel well, trace them to disconnect and remove them.
6   Look inside the area concealed by the spare wheel well. This can be used for storage or fitting a leisure battery, for example. Make sure it's rust protected before fitting any additional panelling.
7   Some holes left by the spare wheel well will need to be covered, especially if they can potentially leak engine or petrol fumes into the interior. Measure up and cut some metal panels to fit in position.
8   The large hole left by the removal of the spare wheel well can be covered with a sheet of metal and additional upholstery. First, measure the size of the hole before cutting out a sheet of metal.
9   A brand-new sheet of metal to cover the hole isn't necessary. An old washing-machine top is ideal for instance. After taking measurements, cut it out and fold over the edges to remove any sharp bits.
10 Refit any existing upholstery (e.g. the rear part of the bed) and measure the gap that needs to be filled.

TOOLBOX

- Centre punch
- Chisel
- Electric drill with drill bits 4–10mm
- Goggles and gloves
- Hacksaw
- Hammer
- Pop rivet gun and rivets
- Screwdrivers
- Staple gun

Difficulty level: 3/5
On your own? Yes
Time: 4–6 hours

This gap could be filled with a foam base to help widen the bed for example. Take measurements and draw an overhead view of the gap to fill.
11 Foam can be ordered to size from most upholstery suppliers (check it's the same thickness as the rest of the bed). This can be covered with a suitable material and a thin hardboard base measured and cut to attach the material to it. Roughly cut a piece of material and assemble it with the foam and hardboard.
12 Using a staple gun, secure the ends of the material to the underside of the hardboard. This is a simple and quick method of making your own upholstery. The underside of the hardboard won't be visible.

13 When securing the material to the hardboard, fold the corners before stapling them. This will help to achieve a neat finish, although the corners probably won't be visible as they are concealed by the rest of the bed.

14 After making the additional upholstery to fill the gap left by the removal of the spare wheel well, trial fit it and make sure the material is pulled tight with no creases or imperfections showing.

15 Check the new inserts fit flush with the rest of the bed and don't look out of place. It's impossible to conceal the gaps between the inserts and the bed unless a cover is placed over all of them which, when using the bed will be the case anyway.

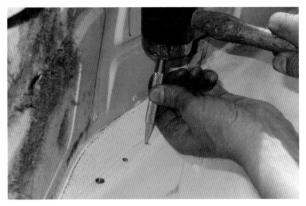

Centre punch any spot welds before drilling them out.

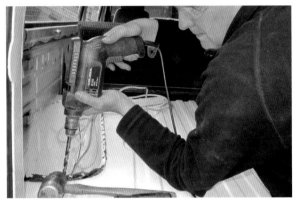

Drill through the first layer of metal to dislodge the spot welds.

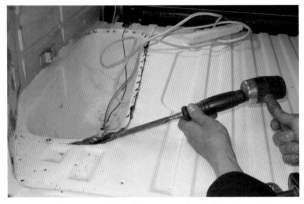

Don't expect the spare wheel well to pop out after drilling through its spot welds. Lever it out with a chisel.

A hacksaw comes in useful for cutting through hard-to-access areas.

Watch your fingers on those sharp edges when removing the spare wheel well.

The space underneath the spare wheel well is often a useful storage area.

Panelling is essential here to isolate any fumes from the petrol tank.

Measure the hole left by the removal of the spare wheel well before cutting a suitable sized panel to cover it.

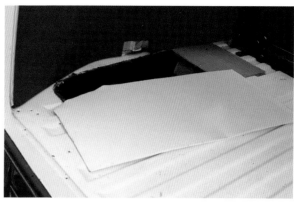

This panel was cut out of a washing machine top. Its edges are sharp, so they have been folded over.

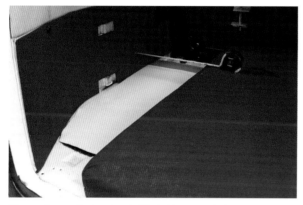

Measure the gap that needs to be filled with more upholstery.

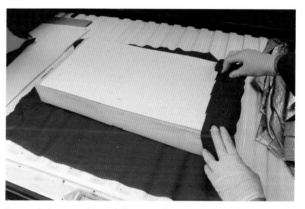

Extra upholstery can be made from matching material with foam and a hardboard base.

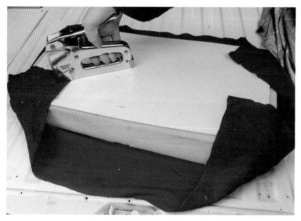

Stapling material onto a hardboard base is a quick method of making an insert for the bed mattress.

The corners need to be folded over and tucked in when stapling the material to the hardboard. It's like wrapping a gift.

The two completed inserts are pushed into position to check they fit flush.

The completed rear bed with enough additional width for a small child. Much better than sleeping next to a spare wheel.

seats and sleeping

The seating and sleeping area of a camper van are one of the major features and requirements. This chapter shows how to repair and fit seats, add extra beds and make your own seats.

HOW TO REMOVE SEATS FROM OTHER VEHICLES

Using seats from other vehicles and fitting them into a camper van is often a cheap solution to acquiring a good-quality seat for very little money.

Leather seats, for example, can be found in the majority of vehicles and many camper van owners have found ways of fitting them. Seats from MPVs and similar vehicles often have swivel bases, arm rests and several adjustments.

Fitting a seat from another vehicle into a camper van isn't always as straightforward as it may seem. The first hurdle involves measuring up to see whether the seat will actually fit and the doors can be closed. Next, you

need to work out how the seat can be secured safely inside the camper van.

We'll start with the basics of removing a seat, which is outlined in the following steps, then progress to stripping and repairing seats, before showing how to fit them.

1 Most front seats are secured to the centre tunnel and side sills with bolts. Slide the seat fully forward and back to look for these mounting bolts, then undo them.

These front and rear seats from a Mk1 Golf GTi are light and unsophisticated, making them a potential donor for a camper van.

TOOLBOX

- Spanners and socket set

Difficulty level: 1/5
On your own? Yes
Time: 1–2 hours

2 If the seat is equipped with a seatbelt tensioner or airbag, look underneath it for its electrical connector plugs and disconnect them. Make sure the vehicle's ignition is off and don't use any metal objects to disconnect them – they may short out and activate.

3 If possible, tilt the back of the seat forwards when removing the seat to make it less awkward to manoeuvre. Watch the seat runners don't scratch the paintwork on the car.

4 Rear seats can also be used in many camper vans. They usually consist of a seat back and base. The base is often secured at the front and can usually be pulled out forwards.

5 The rear seat back on many cars folds forward, so it's often straightforward to detach it from the top. At the base however, there may be mounting bolts or a particular procedure for dismantling it.

Most seats are secured on runners to the centre tunnel and sills.

Be careful when detaching air bag and seatbelt tensioner plugs. Static and metal objects can short them out and activate them.

Fold the seat-back forwards to remove it and watch the runners on the paintwork.

Rear seats usually consist of a base and a back. The base is often secured at the front and in some cases can be pulled free.

This rear seat-back from a BMW MINI needs to be detached in the middle to remove all of it.

In some cases, the back and base of a rear seat need to be removed together, such as on this Mk1 Golf GTi.

HOW TO STRIP AND RECOVER A SEAT

If you intend to use seats from another car and fit them into a camper van, then you may find some second-hand bargains, but they may be damaged and in need of recovering. In many cases, made-to-measure seat covers are available and they are relatively straightforward to fit. Seat covers are often constructed in a similar manner to clothing, such as a pullover or jumper. They can be removed and fitted by pulling them over the seat's framework and padding.

There are a few potential complications when it comes to removing and fitting seat covers. Modern seats have a number of controls, airbags and tensioner systems, which need to be carefully removed. Airbags and tensioners can be dangerous, especially if they are accidentally activated, so make sure you know how to remove them correctly and safely. Controls such as tilt and reclining mechanisms often don't need to be removed, but some parts of it may need to be taken off the seat to be able to remove the cover. Similarly, some parts may need to be repaired, such as a broken release wire that tilts the back of the seat.

1 Plastic covers and controls may obstruct the removal of the seat covers, so these will need to be removed first. Plastic trim can often be removed with a trim tool.
2 Seat controls for sliding, reclining and adjusting may need to be removed before the seat covers can be removed. If something looks difficult to remove, try prising off a cover using a screwdriver and you may find some fixings underneath it.

Plastic covers on the edge of the seat can usually be removed with a trim tool.

This seat base height-adjuster looks difficult to remove, but once the small cover has been removed …

… it all becomes more obvious and there's a Torx bolt underneath that secures the lever.

Large plastic covers are often clipped in place, but can be awkward to remove.

Examine the base of the seat back to see if the bottom of the cover is attached to the seat base cover.

Plastic fittings may need to be released that secure the seat cover to the seat frame.

3 Some plastic trim is simply clipped in position and needs lots of persuasion to remove it. Use a trim tool to help lever it off and look out for other fixings that may be obstructing its removal.

4 Whilst the seat covers for the seat back and base are often separate, they may be attached to help keep them tight. Look at the bottom of the seat back to see if there are any fittings.

5 Seat covers are often secured to the seat frame and padding using hog rings, which are best removed using hog-ring pliers. These rings are sharp and can cut your fingers.

6 The seat cover can be lifted off the base and seat back in the same manner as removing a pullover or jumper from your body. You may find the padding comes off at the same time.

7 New seat covers need to be stretched over the seat's padding and secured with new fittings, such as hog rings, in the original locations.

8 Check the seat covers are evenly fitted and there are no sags or unwanted creases. Take your time, making sure the cover is correctly fitted.

9 Holes may need to be cut in the new seat covers for the headrests and other items that are attached to the seat. Use a sharp knife to make clean cuts through the material.

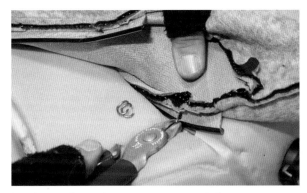

Hog rings are often used to secure a seat cover to the frame and padding.

The cover on the seat back can usually be lifted up and off.

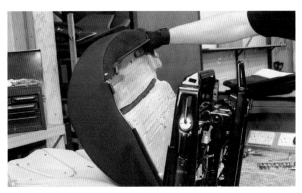

The padding and seat base's cover may have to be removed together before separating them.

Hog-ring pliers are essential for fitting new hog rings to secure a seat cover.

Make sure the new seat cover is a tight fit and its pattern is correctly aligned.

Cutting holes for headrests can be a scary experience.

HOW TO RETRIM A HEADREST

Headrests are the smallest item on a seat to retrim, but they can also be the most awkward. If an old cover is already fitted, it will probably be secured at the base with a zip or a long plastic clip. Once released, the old cover can be peeled or lifted off. Fitting the new cover is a little more difficult, partly because it will probably be a tight fit and also because you don't want to tear the fabric. The following steps outline what's involved.

1   Some headrests consist of foam padding with a cover around it. If this is the case, then look at the underneath of the headrest to see if the cover can be unzipped or unclipped.
2   After unclipping or unzipping a headrest cover, manoeuvre it up and off the headrest padding. If there's no indication of how to remove the cover, the new one can usually be fitted over it.
3   Try turning the new headrest cover inside out, then line it up on top of the headrest and work it down and over. This can be awkward and

Look underneath the headrest to see if the cover is zipped or clipped.

The old headrest cover may tear upon removal.

Turn the new cover inside out before fitting it.

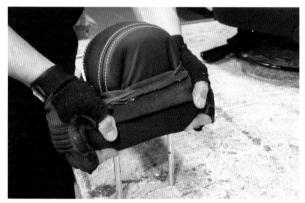

Fitting the new headrest cover can be awkward. Be careful not to tear it.

The bottom of the cover may need cutting to fit around the headrest's legs.

Clipping together the base of the headrest cover achieves a tight fit.

will take roughly five minutes to complete.

4 Be careful not to tear the new cover as you work it into position. Watch the cover around the opening to make sure it's not overstretched and starting to rip.

5 Once the cover is over the headrest, it probably won't be straight, so will need working around with your fingers and thumbs. The bottom of the cover may need to be cut to fit it around the legs.

6 Clip or zip the opening in the base of the cover. Clips consisting of two plastic strips can be very fiddly to join together, so use a trim tool to help.

HOW TO RETRIM A REAR SEAT

Rear seats are often less complicated to retrim than front seats. They are usually a simple design with the cover being secured at the back or base using hog rings and plastic clips. Once undone, the cover can be pulled up and off the rear seat back or base and a new one fitted.

1 Rear seat covers may be clipped in position. Look around the back of the seat back and base for clips that are attached to metal rods. These are usually straightforward to detach.

2 The rear seat covers are also usually secured with hog rings, which need to be removed and discarded using a pair of hog-ring pliers.

3 If you cannot see any clips or hog rings, try prising the trim on the back of the seat to see if it can be released.

4 If headrests are fitted, you may need to remove the plastic guide plugs for their legs, which will obstruct the removal of the seat cover from the top of the seat back.

5 Once all of the fixings and obstructions have been removed from the

TOOLBOX

• Flatblade screwdrivers
• Hog-ring pliers
• Spanners and socket set
• Trim tool (or tack lifter from hardware shop)

Difficulty level: 1/5
On your own? Yes
Time: 2–3 hours

rear seat, its cover can be removed. Avoid tearing or cutting the seat cover, as you may need it to make a new one.

6 Some seat covers can be manoeuvred over the seat's foam and padding, slipping it on like a pullover or jumper. However, it will still have some clips or other fittings to keep it in position.

7 If the seat covers are fitted with hog rings, use new ones, if possible, and use a pair of hog-ring pliers to fit them.

Plastic clips are often used to secure the seat cover to the seat.

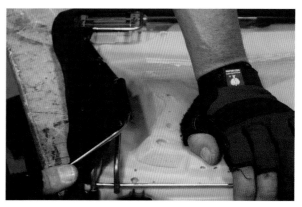

These long, plastic clips can be prised off with a screwdriver.

Hog rings are often used to keep a cover tight-fitting and can be found by turning part of it inside out.

If the seat looks as though it's sealed, try levering the edges with a screwdriver or trim tool.

Remove any plastic locating plugs for the headrests.

Make sure all fittings are removed before attempting to remove the cover.

Sometimes a new cover can be fed over the original foam for the seat.

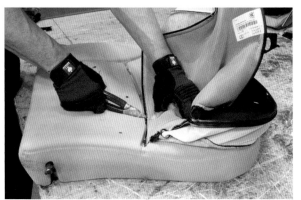

Use new hog rings to refit the cover and keep it firmly in position.

HOW TO RESTORE A LEATHER SEAT

Second-hand seats are a cheap solution for a camper van's interior, especially leather seats from a Saab, Mazda MX-5 or similar car. These can often be found through the classifieds in motoring magazines and club websites or on auction websites such as eBay. Quite often, however, used leather seats have signs of wear and tear, with cracks in the leather finish and scuff marks around the edges (bolsters). Fortunately, the majority of damage and wear can be repaired using a DIY kit or a specialist.

In brief, restoring a leather seat involves cleaning as much of the dirt off it as possible, filling in any cracks or scuff marks before applying a colour pigment and finishing off with a lacquer to seal it.

DIY leather restoration kits are ideal for leather seats with straight colours, such

as black, but not so easy for browns and reds. A colour match for a brown leather seat isn't as easy to achieve as black, so you may find the finish on a brown seat is darker or lighter than you wanted.

The following steps show leather-restoration specialist Leather Revive (www. LeatherRevive.co.uk) tackling the cracks and scuff marks on a leather seat from a Mazda MX-5, which is ideal for fitting inside a camper van.

1   Any areas of the seat that don't need to be treated, such as the recliner controls and other plastic parts, should be protected with masking tape to prevent them from being discoloured with pigment and filler.

2   Clean the seats with a nylon nail-brush and some leather-cleaning fluid. This helps to remove engrained dirt that will prevent the new paint/pigment from sticking to the leather.

3   Wipe over the seat with a micro-fibre cloth to help remove any dirt and residue that was removed in the last step. Steps 2 and 3 may need to be repeated a few times.

4   Scotchbrite with leather-cleaning fluid helps to remove stubborn marks. The scouring action of the Scotchbrite is more abrasive than a nylon brush.

5   Any deep marks that cannot be removed with the nylon brush or Scotchbrite can often be removed

TOOLBOX

- Breathing mask
- Colour pigment, glue and leather filler
- Spatula
- Hair-dryer
- Leather-cleaning fluid
- Masking tape
- Micro-fibre cloths
- Nylon nail-brush
- Scotchbrite
- Spray equipment and small compressor
- Wet and dry paper (P400)

Difficulty level: 3/5
On your own? Yes
Time: from 2 hours

Mask off any parts of the seat that don't want to be restored.

Clean the seat with leather-cleaning fluid and a nylon nail-brush.

Wipe off any residue with a micro-fibre cloth.

Scotchbrite helps to remove more dirt.

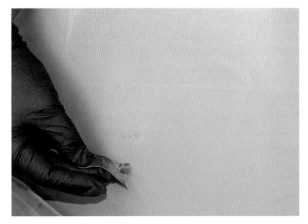

Engrained dirt can often be removed with P400 wet and dry paper.

Scuff marks and cracks need to be filled.

Mixing the pigment is where a specialist excels.

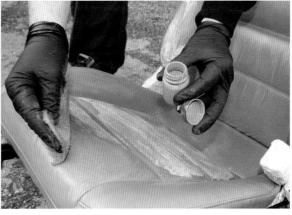

Apply the pigment with a Scotchbrite pad and rub it in.

Cracks can be filled with pigment.

After the pigment has dried, key it before the final coat.

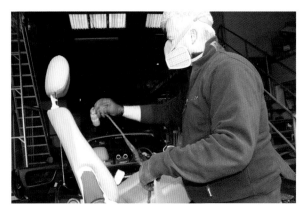

Spray a mixture of pigment and lacquer for a sealed finish.

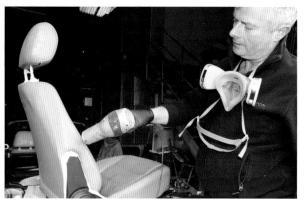

A hair-dryer can be used to dry the pigment, filler and the top coat.

with P400 grade wet and dry paper. Despite the fact that the abrasive action of the wet and dry leaves a rough finish, it will be covered with pigment.

6 Scuff marks and cracks can be filled with a combination of leather glue and leather filler. This helps to build the leather back up. The glue helps to stick the filler to the leather. It must be dry before being smoothed off with wet and dry paper.

7 Most DIY leather-seat restoration kits will be supplied with a colour that hopefully matches the seat that is being repaired. A specialist such as Leather Revive, however, has the skill and experience to mix an accurate colour match.

8 Apply the pigment with a clean Scotchbrite pad, which helps to gently rub it into the leather. Difficult sections, such as piping, can be coloured using a small spatula from a craft shop.

9 Some of the cracks in the leather may require a few coats of pigment. However, the pigment can also be used as a sort of filler, applying it with a spatula to help to fill the cracks.

10 Once the pigment has dried, the repair can be assessed to see whether it has adequately covered the leather. If it has, the leather needs to be rubbed down with wet and dry to help key the finish for the final coat.

11 The final coat is sprayed on and consists of a mixture of pigment and lacquer. It helps to provide a sealed finish. A mask must be worn when spraying.

12 The wet pigment and lacquer is dried off using a hair-dryer (a heat-gun can also be used). This helps to shorten the drying time and assess the results of the repair. A few top coats may be required.

HOW TO FIT SEATS FROM ANOTHER VEHICLE

Camper vans often have the space to be creative when it comes to seating, enabling you to source some plush seats from another vehicle and make them fit. The work involved can be straightforward, but is very often time-consuming and more difficult than you expect it to be. Safety is a very important issue when it comes to fitting seats and it must be stressed that seats need to be securely fitted to the structural parts of a camper van. They need to remain secure in the event of an accident with no risk of breaking free and causing injury.

There are a number of methods of mounting a seat into a camper van. In most cases, the original mounting points will not line up with anything inside your camper van, especially where a seat has been removed from a completely different vehicle. It's usually best to remove any unwanted framework from the donor seats and make your own. The following steps show how to do this with lengths of angled (channelled) aluminium. There are also universal seat runners that can be purchased from seat stockists, which are far better and safer than attempting to make your own, should you need an adjustable seat.

This rear seat from a Ford Escort could make a perfect seat in the front of a camper van, but it must be securely fitted and not pose a risk of injury in the event of an accident.

1   Look at the framework on the donor seat to see if it can be fitted into the camper van and its mounting points used. In some cases this may be possible, but it is often rare. Instead, a new framework usually needs to be created.

2   Clean the area where the seat will be fitted, checking for corroded metal, which must be repaired, and making sure all of the area is structurally sound. The seat must be mounted to areas where the original seats are fitted, such as crossmembers and sills.

3   Trial fit the donor seat and make sure there's sufficient headroom when you are seated and that you can reach the steering wheel and pedals. Some seats may be too tall or too wide.

4   Look at the base of the seat to see if there are any mounting holes or

Finding a seat with a suitable mounting frame is rare. Often, you have to make your own.

Make sure the metalwork around and under the seat is strong and rot free.

Check the seating position isn't too high or offset from the controls.

Look for mounting points on the underside of the seat and take measurements.

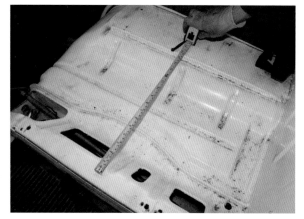

Measure the space available to fit the seat.

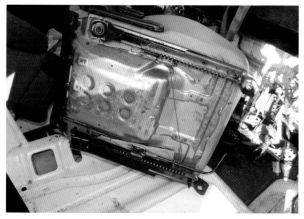

This MX-5 seat has an awkward mounting frame that's difficult to use in a camper van.

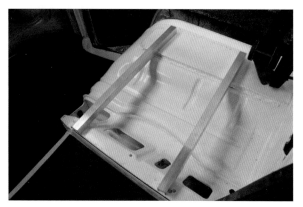

Lengths of channelled aluminium are useful for making a flat framework for mounting a seat.

Measure the mounting points on the underside of the seat to see where to drill holes in the new framework.

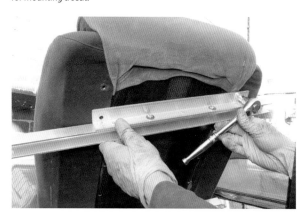

Make sure the mounting brackets are securely fitted together.

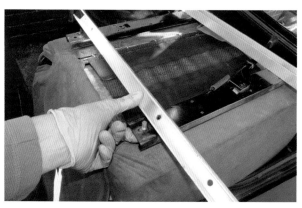

Universal seat runners are available from many seat stockists. Don't try making your own.

Check the doors will close before mounting the seats in position.

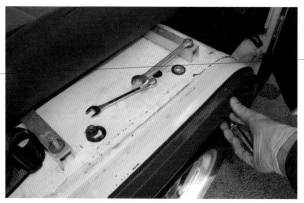

Use M10 bolts with large washers and nylock nuts to secure the seat to the camper van.

points that can be used to fit to the camper van or onto a new frame. Take measurements to see if these are suitable for using inside the camper van.

5   Measure the area inside the camper van where the donor seats can be fitted. Use the measurements made in the last step to calculate whether the seat can be securely fitted. You may find some of the mounting holes on the seats cannot be used.

6   If the base of the seat has a complicated mounting frame, you may want to consider trying to remove it and fitting either a universal frame/slider or making your own. Universal seat frames are available, but the next steps show how to make your own.

7   It can be straightforward to make your own framework using lengths of channelled aluminium. They can form a flat surface and there's space to mount them to the underside of a seat and to the camper van.

8   Many seats have threaded mounting holes on the underside, which can be used to mount a new framework. If this is the case, measure up, drill holes in the channelled aluminium and secure it to the underside of the seat with bolts.

9   It may be difficult to use a length of channelled aluminium to secure to the underside of a seat and the camper van, as all the holes may not line up. In such a case, securely attach extra pieces, but make sure they are firmly fixed with bolts and rivets.

10 If you'd like a seat to be adjustable, ready-made universal runners can often be fitted between the base of the seat and the framework. Don't forget this adds height to the seat and so reduces headroom.

11 With the framework firmly fitted onto the base of the seat, trial fit the seat inside the camper van and make sure the doors can be closed. Check once more that the seating position is suitable, especially for the driver.

12 When you have determined the exact position of each seat, look for suitable mounting points and drill holes through the framework and camper van. Fit M10 bolts with large washers and nylock nuts.

HOW TO FIT SEATBELTS

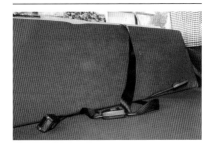

There are a number of seatbelt kits available for camper vans, which can be bought from specialists and general seatbelt stockists. These range from the simple lap belt and three-point belt, up to inertia reel seatbelts and four-point harnesses.

In brief, fitting a seatbelt involves finding suitable mounting points and securing the seatbelt to these. However, finding suitable mounting points isn't always as straightforward as it may seem. These mounting points need to have been purposely fitted to the camper van and are often easy to identify. Look for threaded holes or captive nuts fitted to structural parts of the camper van, such as a sill, crossmember or strengthening beam. If you have removed some seats and not reused the original mounting points, then these can sometimes be used to secure a seatbelt.

If you cannot find a suitable mounting point for part of a seatbelt, then all is not lost. The simplest solution is to buy a spreader plate, which consists of a square piece of steel with a captive nut welded to the centre. Drill a hole through a thick enough panel in the camper van, fit a bolt and part of the seatbelt on one side and the spreader plate with captive nut on the other. This solution is ideal for fitting seatbelts to wheel arches, but make sure the panel you are using is sufficiently thick. If you are at all unsure, seek professional advice.

For ease of use, inertia reel seatbelts are a favourite because they are self-adjusting. However, they are possibly the most complicated type of seatbelt to fit. The inertia reel unit usually has to be positioned vertically to ensure it doesn't lock when the seatbelt is slowly pulled out. Most inertia reel units have some sort of pendulum lock inside, which moves and traps the seatbelt in the event of a crash or a sharp pull on the seatbelt. If the inertia reel unit isn't mounted vertically, the lock may trap the seatbelt.

Other potential problems that can arise when fitting an inertia reel seatbelt concern the upper mount. This should ideally be fitted at the shoulder height of the passenger, but such a mounting point may not be available or possible to make. Some camper vans have been equipped with an extension bracket to ensure the upper mounting point is at shoulder height, but this may be illegal in your country as it is not directly mounted to the vehicle.

Fitting seatbelts to a camper van must be completed to a high level of safety. So if you are at all unsure about using particular mounting points or how a seatbelt should be fitted, consult a professional and ask them to help you.

TOOLBOX

- Spanners and socket set
- Electric drill and drill bits

Difficulty level: 2/5
On your own? Yes
Time: 2+ hours

A spreader plate can be used where a proper mounting point is not available.

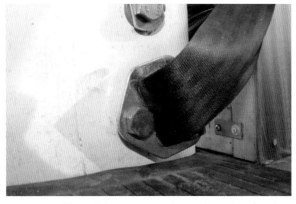

Secure parts of the seatbelt to purpose made mounting points where there are threaded holes or captive nuts.

A spreader plate with a captive nut allows a seatbelt to be mounted to a range of panels.

Mounting the seatbelt to a door's striker plate is possible, but check there are no safety regulations that disallow this.

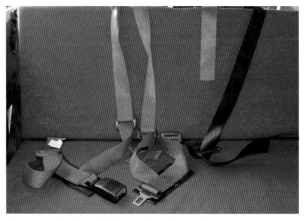

Harnesses and adjustable belts are the easiest to fit.

Inertia reel seatbelts are a favourite. Start by mounting the inertia reel unit.

Adjust the mounting of the inertia reel unit to ensure the seatbelt can be pulled out.

Secure the upper mounting point for the seatbelt to the inside of the camper van.

An extension bracket can help to ensure the seatbelt's upper mounting point is shoulder-height, but check this is allowed in your country.

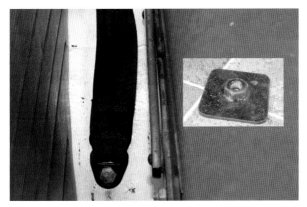

The seatbelt here is fitted to a wheel arch, so a spreader plate has been used.

Underneath this rock-and-roll bed, there are several seatbelt mounts that can be used.

This rear-facing seatbelt uses a mounting point for a front-facing middle seatbelt.

Cable ties are useful for securing seatbelt sockets and stopping them flapping around.

1 All parts of a seatbelt should be secured to purpose-made mounting points, which consist of either a threaded hole in a strengthened section of the bodywork or a captive nut.

2 If part of a seatbelt cannot be fixed to a specific mounting point outlined in the last step, then it is often possible to drill a hole in a panel and fit a spreader plate behind it, which consists of a square of steel with a captive nut.

3 In some cases, a structural mounting point, such as a striker plate for a door, can be used to mount part of a seatbelt, but check this is allowed in your country – safety laws may dictate otherwise.

4 Lap belts and adjustable belts are some of the easiest seatbelts to fit. Even racing harnesses can be fitted, which are all adjustable, but can be a little fiddly at times.

5 Most people prefer inertia reel seatbelts because they are easy to operate. They require three mounting points and the following steps show how to fit them. Start by mounting the inertia reel unit.

6 Make sure the seatbelt can be pulled out and retracted from the inertia reel unit. You may need to adjust it to make sure it is perfectly vertical to stop it locking the belt.

7 Fit an upper mounting point for the seatbelt. This should ideally be higher than a passenger's shoulder, but this is not always possible (*see* the next step for more ideas).

8 It may be possible to make an extension bracket for the upper seatbelt mounting, so that it can be positioned at shoulder height for the passenger. Check this is allowed in your country.

9 The final mount for the inertia reel seatbelt needs to be at the side of the passenger. It could share the inertia reel unit's mount. If a hole needs to be drilled, secure the seatbelt with a spreader plate.

10 Finally, a socket needs to be fitted close to the passenger to attach the seatbelt's buckle. Look for existing mounting points, such as underneath a rock-and-roll bed.

11 Look around existing seatbelt mounts for additional mounting points to fit the seatbelt socket.

You may be able to double up on a mounting point.

12 Seatbelt sockets can get in the way or disappear down the back of seats, so try tying them back with cable ties.

HOW TO MAKE A BUDDY SEAT

A buddy seat is a useful additional piece of furniture inside a camper van. It's often used to make a rearward facing seat that allows an extra person to sit at a table. It also provides useful storage underneath the seat.

There are a number of professional kits available to make fantastic-looking buddy seats. Traditional buddy seats that were fitted in the early camper vans can also be renovated, if you want a retro look. However, for around £20, it is feasible to make your own, although the results may be difficult to match the 'professionals'.

There are a few points to consider when making a buddy seat. It's important to determine how high the seat needs to be to make sure there's sufficient headroom and legroom if you need to sit at a table.

The materials used in the making of the seat frame need to be strong enough to hold a person's weight, but not over-engineered so that they take up all the storage space or add too much weight to the overall camper van. Some older buddy seats certainly look very sturdy, but are also very heavy. The photographs accompanying the following steps show a framework being made from lengths of pine wood and, after testing the finished buddy seat for a couple of years, it was apparent a thinner material could have been used to help create more storage space inside.

Achieving a professional finish for a home-made buddy seat is relatively easy, but you may need to shop around for materials if you want to keep costs to a minimum. The sides of the buddy seat can be covered in hardboard, which

TOOLBOX

- Chipboard for seat base and back
- Fabric for seat covers
- Foam for seat padding
- Hardboard for sides of seat
- Pine or harder wood for seat framework
- Scissors for cutting material
- Screwdrivers
- Staple gun
- Tape-measure

Difficulty level: 2/5
On your own? Yes
Time: 3+ hours

doesn't look particularly attractive, but this can be wrapped in a cheap vinyl (see Chapter 3 for more information on vinyl wrapping panels). The seat base and back can be trimmed in material bought from a local market and stapled to the back of a chipboard base. However, if you can sew or know someone who can, then covers can be made, which look more professional.

1 Measure the area in the camper van where you intend to fit the buddy seat, checking how wide it can be and the height it should be to allow for headroom and legroom at a table. Experiment with boxes to find suitable dimensions.

2 Using the dimensions from the last step, make a square frame from four lengths of wood for the seat base to sit on. This will represent the full width and depth of the buddy seat. Use screws to secure the framework together.

3 The framework made in the last step will probably be quite wobbly, so make or buy some brackets from a DIY shop to help hold it more securely together. Fit the brackets with short screws.

4 Accounting for the height of the framework from the last step and the height of the seat padding, cut four lengths of wood to form the legs of the buddy seat. Secure these onto the base of the framework with screws and L-shaped brackets.

5 The back of the buddy seat will probably face a panel – it won't be visible, so it won't need to be covered, but can be strengthened with a length of wood, secured with screws and brackets.

6 The three exposed sides of the buddy seat (front and two sides) can be covered in hardboard. First, measure the required dimensions of each panel, as the buddy seat may not be perfectly square.

7 The hardboard panels look quite bland if left plain, but they can be painted or wrapped in vinyl. If you intend to paint the hardboard, rub

LEFT: Buddy seats from early camper vans are very retro, but often bulky and heavy.

BELOW: A buddy seat provides useful additional storage space.

it down first with sandpaper to key the surface and help the paint stick to it.

8 Secure the hardboard panels to the sides of the buddy seat using glue or screws. If you want a clean finish, use glue. Make sure each hardboard panel fits flush and won't obstruct the seat or the base of the framework.

9 Once all of the side panels have been fitted, trial fit the half-completed buddy seat inside the camper van and check that the height of the seat padding is sufficient. Also, check that the buddy seat's width and depth are okay.

10 Cut a piece of chipboard for the seat base and back (if required). Purchase seat foam to the same dimensions as the base and back, then cut out a piece of material to cover them. Seat foam and material can be bought from upholstery specialists.

11 Wrap the material around the seat foam and base and staple it onto the back of the chipboard. This can be awkward, so be prepared to remove the staples and start again. Make sure the material is folded at the edges and pulled tight.

12 Fit some wooden blocks to the underneath of the seat base to help locate it when it's fitted to the framework and prevent it sliding around. Trial fit the seat base and back in position with the buddy seat in the camper van.

Measure the space available where the buddy seat can be fitted.

Start with a framework that the seat base will sit on.

Secure the framework with brackets to make it stronger.

Fit legs to the underneath of the framework to create a box for the buddy seat.

If the rear of the buddy seat cannot be seen, it won't need covering, but can be strengthened with a brace.

Measure the dimensions for all of the sides before making them from hardboard or a similar lightweight material.

TOP LEFT: *Hardboard sides look tatty, but can be transformed with retro wood vinyl wrap. It's cheesy, but cheap.*

TOP RIGHT: *The hardboard sides can be secured to the buddy seat framework with screws or glue.*

LEFT: *Here's the finished bottom-half of the buddy seat.*

ABOVE LEFT: *The seat back and base can be made from chipboard, foam padding and material.*

ABOVE RIGHT: *Staple the material to the chipboard of the seat base and back.*

LEFT: *Fit wooden blocks on the bottom of the seat base to stop it sliding around.*

HOW TO RESTORE A ROCK-AND-ROLL BED

Rock-and-roll beds are the ideal solution for rear seating and sleeping. If you have bought a second-hand rock-and-roll bed, or already have one that's starting to look tatty, then restoring it with new foam and fabric is usually quite straight-forward.

The work involved in stripping a rock-and-roll bed and fitting new material isn't usually very difficult, but you may want to find someone with sewing skills to make the new covers. Whilst new material can be simply stretched round and stapled onto a wooden board for the seat base or back of a rock-and-roll bed, a sewn-together cover looks so much better and has less risk of creasing.

This book does not recommend making your own rock-and-roll bed, partly because the safety regulations surrounding seats are complicated. The seating aspect of a rock-and-roll bed needs to be correctly designed so that passengers are not injured in the event of an accident. Consequently, this is beyond the scope of

Rock-and-roll beds can consist of a framework that folds down to make a bed.

TOOLBOX

- Scissors for cutting material
- Sewing machine (optional)
- Sharp knife
- Spanners and screwdrivers
- Spray glue/adhesive
- Staple gun
- Tape-measure

Difficulty level: 3/5
On your own? Yes
Time: weekend job

---

a DIY enthusiast and so it is not recommended you make your own rock-and-roll bed.

Set aside a long weekend to remove, restore and refit a rock-and-roll bed. It's worthwhile sourcing some new foam and most local upholstery suppliers can cut this to size.

1 Remove the rock-and-roll bed. Depending on how it has been fitted inside the camper van, there will probably be a number of fittings secured to the floor and other areas inside.
2 It may be easier to leave the frame-

work of the rock-and-roll bed in position and remove the seat base and back, which are going to be retrimmed.
3 With the seat base and back removed (separate the two if necessary), remove the fabric from them. Do not cut it off, but find out how it is secured. It may be fitted with staples.
4 After removing the fabric from the seat base and back, remove the foam padding. Do not cut up or damage any of these parts as you will need them for templates to make the new material.

Undo all the fittings that secure the rock-and-roll bed inside the camper van.

It may be easier to remove the seat base and seat back separately, leaving the rock-and-roll bed's framework behind.

5   If the foam padding is glued to the seat back or base, carefully cut it off using a sharp knife. Do not cut it off in chunks, try to keep it in one piece to help with ordering new foam padding.

6   Using the old foam, renew it if it is in poor condition or old. Foam upholstery suppliers usually sell made-to-measure foam. Glue the new foam in position to the seat base and back.

7   Take the old fabric for the seat base and back and use this as a template to cut out some new material. If the old fabric has been sewn to form a shape, cut the stitches to make it flat.

8   If you can sew, stitch the new material together to make a tight-fitting cover. If you cannot sew and cannot find someone to do this, you can still proceed to the next step.

9   Fit the new material over the seat base and the seat back. It will be a tight fit if it has been sewn to shape, but loose if it hasn't.

10 Staple the material to the wooden base for the seat base and back.

If the material wasn't sewn to make a shape, make sure it is folded at the corners to avoid leaving unwanted creases on the exposed surface.

11 The exposed wood on the seat back can be covered in any spare material, such as a piece of carpet or some vinyl.

12 Once the seat base and back have been restored, they can be refitted into the camper van. Make sure all fittings are secure and renew any nuts, bolts or screws that look rusty or old.

Remove the old material from the seat base and back. It may be stapled down.

Separate the material and foam from the wooden board of the seat back and base.

If the foam is glued to a wooden board, carefully cut it free.

Glue new foam onto the wooden boards for the seat base and back.

Use the old material as a template to cut out new fabric.

If possible, sew the new material to make covers for the seat base and back.

A sewn-together cover results in fewer creases when it's fitted.

Staple the new material onto the wooden board for the seat base and back.

Carpet or other material can be fitted to the rear of the seat back.

When refitting the restored rock-and-roll bed, use new nuts, bolts and screws.

HOW TO MAKE A LUGGAGE GUARD

Rock-and-roll beds and many other forms of rear seats often have a low back, so if luggage is stored at the very back of the camper van, it can often spill over the seat under heavy braking and could be particularly dangerous in the event of an accident. One solution to such a problem is to fit a luggage guard, which is similar to a dog guard.

Aftermarket luggage guards may be available for your camper van or you

could even buy a universal type and make it fit, but a cheaper approach is to make your own. It may not look as professionally finished as a manufactured luggage guard, but it's relatively straightforward to make and it can be made to the correct size.

The following steps show how to make a luggage guard from two lengths of channelled aluminium and a couple of lengths of threaded bar. Channelled aluminium is a useful material for making seat mounts, kitchen units and frame-

works, so it's always worthwhile buying a few lengths. Metal stockists often sell them in long lengths, but they can be cut down to help with transportation. This material is also for sale through eBay. Threaded bar can be purchased from most DIY stores and is measured according to the diameter of its thread. A 10mm-diameter thread, for example, is called M10, which stands for metric 10mm and will require a nut with a 10mm-diameter hole. This dimension is suitable for building a luggage guard.

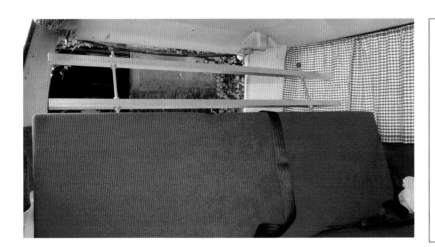

TOOLBOX

- Channelled and angled aluminium
- Electric drill with drill bits
- Hacksaw
- M10 threaded bar with nuts and washers
- Screwdriver and screws
- Tape-measure

Difficulty level: 1/5
On your own? Yes
Time: 1 hour

1 Cut two short (5–8cm) pieces of channelled and angled aluminium and drill 10mm holes through them as shown in the illustration. Mount these pieces onto the back of the seat in two locations using screws (drill 4mm holes through the aluminium).

2 Take a length of threaded bar and make sure it can fit through the two sets of aluminium brackets that were fitted to the back of the seat in the last step. This will be used to secure the luggage guard in position.

3 Measure the width of the rear seat where the luggage guard will be fitted. Cut two lengths of channelled aluminium (three-sided) to match this measurement. These will form the main part of the luggage guard.

4 Leave the threaded bar fitted to the mounting brackets in step 2, then line up the two lengths of channelled aluminium to see where to drill holes through them so they can be fitted onto the threaded bar. Assemble the framework of the luggage guard.

5 Fit nuts and washers along the threaded bar to enable you to adjust the positioning of the channelled aluminium, making sure the framework of the luggage guard is square. If required, fit a nut on the bottom of each threaded bar to lock the luggage guard in position.

Make two sets of mounting brackets for the luggage guard and secure them to the back of the seat.

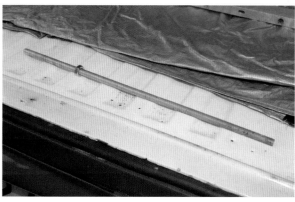

Use two lengths of M10 threaded bar for the vertical sections of the luggage guard.

Slot the threaded bar through the two mounting brackets that are secured to the back of the seat.

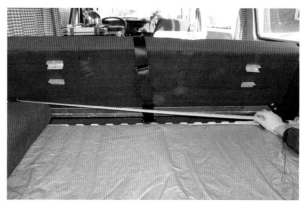

Measure the width of the seat and cut two lengths of channelled aluminium for the horizontal sections of the luggage guard.

Drill holes in the channelled aluminium to create a framework with the threaded bar.

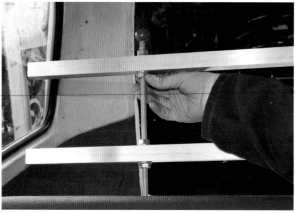

Use a series of nuts and washers to adjust the positioning of the channelled aluminium.

HOW TO FIT A HAMMOCK

The internal width of a camper van is often sufficient for a child to sleep across it. Consequently, there are a number of hammocks available that can be fitted over the front seats to provide extra sleeping space. Most hammocks consist of two metal poles and four brackets, which need to be mounted to the insides of the camper van. The ends of the hammock's poles hook into these brackets to keep it in position. The following nine steps show what's generally involved in fitting a hammock.

TOOLBOX

- Centre punch
- Electric drill with 3mm drill bit
- Hammer
- Marker pen
- Screwdriver

Difficulty level: 2/5
On your own? Easier with a second pair of hands
Time: 2 hours

SAFETY WARNING

When fitting a hammock, avoid fitting the mounting brackets onto fragile surfaces, such as glass, plastic panels or a quarterlight. When using the hammock, don't leave any sharp objects below it and make sure the person using it knows how to safely get on and off it.

1   Take one of the poles for the hammock and find out where it should be fitted to the front of the interior. It will probably be fitted to the inside of the A-pillar. If the width between the pillars differs, depending on where you measure, then you will find there is only one position where the pole can be fitted.

2   Trial fit a mounting bracket for the hammock's pole. This will be secured to the inside of the camper van. In the illustration, the end of the hammock's pole hooks into the bracket. Make sure the hammock's pole can be removed when the bracket is fixed in position.

3   Some brackets are shaped with a larger opening on one side. Make sure this larger opening is at the top of the bracket when fitting it. This will help to hook the end of the hammock's pole into position.

Trial fit one of the hammock's poles to see where it should be located.

4   When you are satisfied you have found the correct position for the mounting brackets, use a marker pen to mark the holes for securing the bracket to the inside of the camper van. Make sure the mounting holes will not go through to any glass.

5   Centre punch the mounting holes that were marked in the last step, then carefully drill these holes using a suitable sized drill bit (3mm in this case and supplied in the kit). Make sure you are not drilling through to glass or other fragile parts.

6   Secure the mounting bracket to the inside of the camper van with screws or whatever is recommended or supplied in the fitting kit. This particular hammock's mounting brackets use screws, which need some force to thread them fully into position.

7   Once both frontmost mounting brackets have been fitted, thread the poles through the hammock and fit one of them in position using the two mounting brackets that have been fitted. Make sure you can manoeuvre the poles in and out of the mounting brackets.

8   Stretch the hammock out and find a suitable location to mount the second pole. You may have to adjust the front seats or remove the headrests. Repeat the steps shown for fitting the mounting brackets.

9   The hammock kit shown here mounts the rearmost brackets on the front doors, so they must be locked when the hammock is in use. When all four mounting brackets have been fitted, carefully fit and test the hammock.

Offer up a mounting bracket to see how it should be fitted.

There's only one way this mounting bracket can be fitted: with the larger opening at the top to locate the hammock's pole.

Mark the holes for securing the mounting bracket.

Carefully drill the holes for the mounting bracket, making sure you don't drill through any glass.

Make sure the mounting brackets are securely fitted as they need to hold the hammock in position.

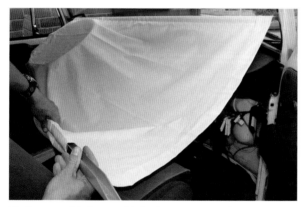

The front part of the hammock is fitted, now move onto the rear.

Find a suitable location to mount the rear of the hammock, away from any glass.

This hammock is secured to the front doors, so they must be locked when it is being used.

kitchen equipment

Catering inside a camper van can be as simple or as sophisticated as you want it to be. This chapter shows how to install an assortment of equipment, ranging from a table and fridge to making your own kitchen pod.

COOKING OPTIONS

Cooking is one of the essential aspects of a camper van and the range of equipment varies from a straightforward single gas stove to ovens, grills and multi-ring hobs.

The majority of options for cooking are operated using gas, although equipment such as toasters, kettles, coffee-makers and ovens largely use mains supplied electricity.

Gas-operated stoves and similar equipment must be installed correctly to ensure there are no gas leaks and risk of fire. If a large gas bottle is being used, make sure it is securely installed on the floor of the camper van, with no risk of it moving around. Retaining-straps are available from camping specialists, which allow the gas bottle to be secured to a structural panel inside the camper van.

A gas bottle installed inside a camper van must have some form of ventilation to ensure that, in the event of a gas leak, the unwanted gas can escape. In most cases, gas is heavier than air, so drill some holes in the floor of the camper van, next to where the gas bottle is installed and fit a plastic vent cover for a neat finish.

Gas stoves can be very simple and compact, and some require very little installation work. The range of compact portable stoves that operate from a small gas canister can often be installed

This portable camping stove is tucked away inside a cupboard and mounted to a panel that slides up and out.

inside a camper van. They are not as powerful as a full-sized stove when it comes to cooking, but they take up less room and can be removed to cook outside. As the photographs that accompany this section illustrate, a portable stove can be built into the furniture of a camper van in a more compact manner than a full-sized stove.

At the opposite end of the scale, a professionally made stove/hob from the likes of Dometic, Spinflo and Smev provide the best finish and the best heat for cooking, but they are not as cheap as the aforementioned ideas. Budget for around £200 or more for a one- or two-ring hob, which can be inset into a worktop or kitchen pod.

If you don t want to spend a three-figure sum on a hob, then a cheaper solution is to buy a two-ring camping stove for around £30 and install it inside a kitchen pod or on top of a kitchen worktop. The following steps explain how to do this.

1   A simple camping stove can be secured to a kitchen worktop inside a camper van and used for cooking food. The first step is to secure a

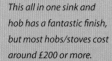

This all in one sink and hob has a fantastic finish, but most hobs/stoves cost around £200 or more.

Secure a hose/pipe to the gas stove. Only use a purpose-made hose intended for attaching to a gas stove.

Some stoves have mounting holes, so drill through to the worktop, but make sure there are no pipes or controls in the way.

These coach bolts have a domed head, which creates a neat finish when they are used to secure the stove to the worktop.

Use washers and nuts to secure the bolts and keep the stove firmly fixed to the worktop.

length of hose between the stove and the gas bottle. Only use hose that is recommended for this purpose.

2 Some stoves have mounting holes at the sides. These can be used to in turn drill holes through a worktop to mount the stove. If there are no mounting holes in the stove, look underneath it to see if new ones can be drilled without damaging any pipes or controls.

3 Once you have at least a couple of mounting holes drilled for your stove, source some bolts that are long and large enough to fit through the stove and worktop. The head of the bolt will be visible, so you may want to choose a domed or allen key head.

4 Secure the end of the bolts fitted in the last step with washers and nuts from underneath the worktop. Route the hose from the stove to the gas bottle, making sure it cannot get trapped or damaged.

FLYING STOVE

The purpose of securing a stove to a worktop is to make sure it doesn't launch itself at any passengers in the event of heavy braking or an accident. So the base of the stove can be bolted down to a worktop, but the metal grille that sits on top is usually slotted in position and can easily be removed. This must be removed and stored in a cupboard when travelling.

HOW TO INSTALL A GAS STOVE UNDER A WORKTOP

Fitting a gas stove/hob so that it is concealed inside a kitchen unit and covered by a lid can be potentially dangerous. Professionally manufactured hobs and stoves that are built for this purpose have a gas cut-off switch for when the lid is closed. This not only reduces the risk of a gas ring setting fire to the lid, but also filling the inside of the camper van with gas.

If you are installing a camping stove inside a kitchen unit, then the first issue to address is fireproofing the surrounding area. Most kitchen units are made from wood, so a firewall needs to be constructed around the stove using sheet metal. The following steps show how to do this using sheet aluminium, which can be purchased from a sheet-metal supplier and cut with a pair of tin snips or a hacksaw.

The underside of the lid that covers the stove also needs to be fireproof. If you already have a wooden lid as part of the kitchen unit's worktop, then it can be lined underneath with sheet metal. Considering this area will only be visible when the lid is raised, it can be lined with cheap material, such as baking trays (the thick metal type, not aluminium foil), which are available from most supermarkets and discount shops for less than the price of sheet metal.

One of the dangers of cooking is liquids boiling over and spills. Consider where that liquid will go if it escapes out of a pan, onto the stove and beyond. Make sure the area is sealed from any electrics to avoid liquid spilling onto them.

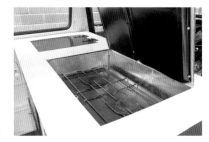

1 Once you have found a suitable location for the stove, a good starting point is to determine how to box it in using a non-flammable material such as sheet aluminium. Using a wooden framework for the base, measure and cut a piece of aluminium that can sit at the back of the stove.

2 Work out how to secure the base for the stove to the sheet aluminium that was cut in the last step. Clamp the aluminium to the framework of the kitchen unit it will be fitted to – this will help to determine how the stove can be boxed in.

3 Drill 4mm holes through the sheet aluminium to allow screws to the fitted through it and into the wooden base for the stove or the framework of the kitchen unit. Use a large 8–10mm drill bit to remove any burrs.

4 Secure the aluminium sheet to the wooden base using 4 × 25mm screws. Secure each part of the wooden base with one screw, then trial fit the assembled framework to check it sits straight before fitting more screws.

5 Place the newly assembled framework in position and temporarily secure it to the kitchen unit with a couple of screws to make sure it can be fitted and it doesn't obstruct anything. There are more parts to fit, so don't fit too many screws yet.

6 Remove the framework, then measure and cut two sheets of aluminium that will form the sides. Drill holes through the sheet and secure them to the wood base with screws.

7 Fit the framework back in position inside the kitchen unit and fit the stove, making sure the pipe between it and the gas bottle doesn't foul anything.

8 The underside of the worktop cover that sits over the stove must be fireproof or resistant to heat. If the cover is made from wood or plastic, fit sheet metal or baking trays to protect it from the heat of the stove.

9 Secure the worktop cover with hinges and decide a method of opening it, such as drilling a finger hole. Worktops are covered in more depth later in this chapter.

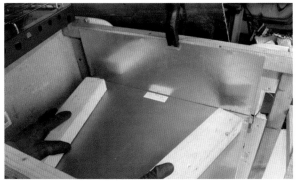

The two lengths of wood can be used as a base for the stove. The aluminium sheet that's temporarily clamped is a back wall for the stove.

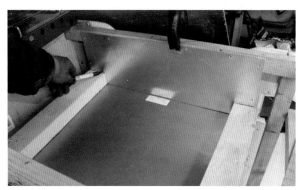

Mark where the wooden base should be fitted to the back wall.

Drill holes through the aluminium sheet to be able to secure it with screws to the wooden base for the stove and the kitchen unit.

Secure the back wall to the stove's wooden base using small screws.

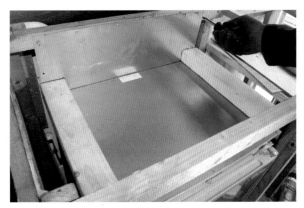

Fix the framework in position, securing it with screws to the kitchen unit.

Cut two lengths of sheet aluminium to form the sides and fix them to the wooden base of the framework.

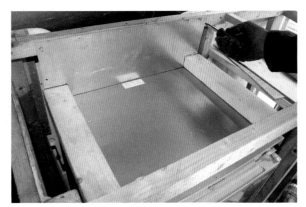

Lower the framework into position inside the kitchen unit.

Fit the stove on to the framework, checking the hose to the gas bottle isn't obstructed.

Line the underneath of the worktop cover with metal to protect it from heat from the stove.

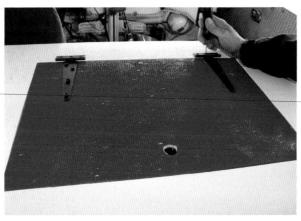

Secure the worktop cover for the stove to the worktop with hinges or catches.

KEEPING FOOD COOL

There are some cheap and expensive solutions to keeping food chilled inside a camper van, ranging from a coolbag filled with ice blocks to a three-way fridge that runs on gas, the vehicle's battery or mains electricity. All of these approaches have their advantages and disadvantages, which are explained in the following list.

◆ Coolbag: Cheap and simple solution, but only suitable for a day unless you can replenish a couple of freezer blocks to keep the temperature inside the bag low. Limited space, but useful for a day trip where frozen food can be used as freezer blocks.

◆ Portable coolbox: Operated via mains electricity or the vehicle's battery. Cheaper models only reduce the ambient temperature, so don't expect an inside temperature of 4°C when it's blazing sunshine and in the thirties. Less overall space than a coolbag, but slightly more effective.

◆ Fridge: The best solution to keeping food cool. Cheaper models are known as fridge boxes, where food is packed inside and the fridge uses mains electricity or the vehicle's battery to operate. More expensive models look like conventional fridges, but will run on electricity (main and vehicle), plus gas such as butane that's used for cooking. Make sure such a fridge can be run on gas inside a camper van (a flue is required). Some portable leisure fridges need to be stored outside when operating on gas.

A full-sized fridge is the best solution for long-term camping and keeping a plentiful supply of chilled food.

A coolbag is useful for a day trip and can be packed with frozen food that will eventually thaw out.

Cheap coolboxes reduce the ambient temperature, so don't expect chilled food if the flagstones are cracking.

HOW TO FIT A FRIDGE

A fridge is one of the bulkiest and potentially heaviest objects that will be fitted inside a camper van, especially when it is packed full of food and drink. Consequently, it needs to be sufficiently secured to the vehicle to make sure it doesn't fall over under cornering or heavy braking.

Some camper van fridges are equipped with mounting brackets or mounting holes. Look around the sides of the fridge for mounting brackets and check the fridge's instruction manual. Look inside the fridge for mounting holes at the sides, which may be covered by plastic discs. These plastic discs will need to be removed to access the mounting holes.

If a fridge has no mounting points, then the work involved in fitting it can be difficult. One solution is to use a ratchet strap for securing objects to roof racks. This can be secured to any mounting points fitted to the floor (you may have to fit your own).

Fridges create heat around the rear and that heat needs to be removed to help avoid overheating. If the back of the fridge is covered, or the entire fridge is enclosed by worktops and cupboards, then vents should be fitted over the back of it. Additional vents can be fitted at the front or sides to provide extra air flow.

If the fridge can be run on gas (the same gas bottle used for cooking), then it must be equipped with a flue to extract waste gases and vent them outside. Specific flue kits are available with most fridges and it is essential these must be used and fitted.

Some gas fridges are not designed to be used inside a camper van. Portable leisure fridges are often half the price of a purpose-made camper van or caravan fridge, and whilst both can

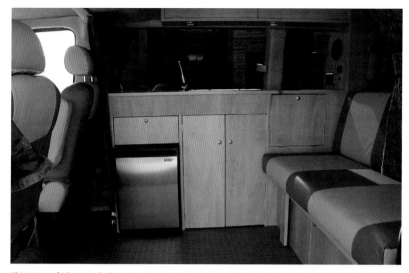

This Waeco fridge may be boxed in by cupboards, but it still needs to be securely mounted to prevent it moving.

The heat generated by a fridge needs to be extracted, so if it is enclosed, fit vents at the front and back.

be operated on gas, a portable fridge has no means of extracting the waste gases in an enclosed area. Such a fridge is only designed to be run on gas if it is stored outside, so do not attempt to run it on gas inside a camper van.

The following steps show how to secure a fridge inside a camper van if it isn't equipped with mounting holes or brackets. The steps show how to remove parts of the fridge to check that new mounting brackets can be fitted. Make sure this is possible with the fridge you are fitting and, if you are unsure about any of the work covered, seek professional advice first.

1   Look around the sides and top of the fridge for a panel that can be used to fit a mounting bracket. You need to be sure that when drilling holes for mounting brackets, you don't damage the fridge.

2   If possible, remove any panels on the fridge. The top panel, for instance, may be secured with screws, so make sure the fridge is switched off and carefully remove it. Check it is safe to do this by consulting the fridge's user manual or manufacturer.

3   Once a panel has been removed, you will be able to see if it can be fitted with a mounting bracket. Make sure any mounting brackets are fitted to corners or edges of a panel where they are stronger.

4   Mounting brackets can be fitted to panels using pop rivets. Drill a suitable hole (usually 4–5mm), then

secure the mounting bracket with a pop rivet. Check the back of the pop rivet doesn't foul anything when the panel is refitted.

5 Try undoing any screws or bolts on the body of the fridge to see if they can be used to fit a mounting bracket. Don't drill any new holes into the fridge as you may cause irreparable damage.

6 Once the mounting brackets are in position on the fridge and any panels are refitted, the next stage is to determine how to use them inside the camper van. A second mounting bracket could be fitted to a panel, for example.

7 If a second mounting bracket needs to be fitted to a panel inside the camper van, secure it with one pop rivet, then make sure the mounting bracket on the fridge is correctly positioned to bolt the two together, before fitting a second pop rivet.

8 If you don't want to fit mounting brackets inside your camper van, then several plastic cable ties could be used to secure the fridge in position. Do not tie them around the components at the back of the fridge, tie them around the brackets fitted to the fridge.

Look around the fridge for suitable locations to fit mounting brackets, but do not drill through the fridge unless you know it's safe to do so.

Some panels can be removed from the fridge, such as the top, if it is secured with screws.

Do not remove panels from the fridge until you have checked the fridge's user guide or with its manufacturer.

Fit mounting brackets to strong sections of a panel, such as a corner or edge.

Carefully drill holes for the mounting bracket.

Pop rivet the mounting bracket to the panel.

It may be possible to fit a mounting bracket with an existing screw, but do not drill any new holes.

Fitting mounting brackets inside the camper van allows any mounting brackets on the fridge to be used.

Fit a mounting bracket to the camper van with one pop rivet, bolt the fridge's mounting bracket to it, then fit a second pop rivet.

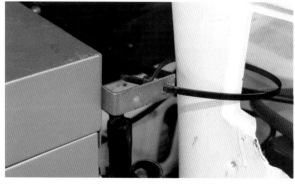

Plastic cable ties can be used to secure a fridge, but you will need a few to ensure the fridge is stable.

HOW TO MAKE A
KITCHEN WORKTOP

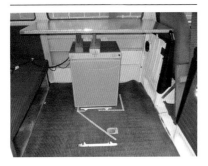

A camper van's kitchen worktop doesn't need to be a complicated design or sophisticated structure. It can be something as simple as a sheet of aluminium or wood that's secured in position. The following steps show how a cheap piece of unwanted aluminium chequer plate can be used to create a worktop. Using cheap materials often means the finish is poor and amateurish, but such surfaces can either be painted or wrapped in a colourful vinyl.

Weight is an issue with a camper van's interior and whilst some equipment cannot be light, panels can be. However, they may need to be braced to prevent them being too flimsy – a worktop that sinks in the middle would look ridiculous.

The total cost of all the materials shown in the following steps came to a mere £25 (£20 for the aluminium chequer plate and £5 for the vinyl that was found on eBay).

1   Decide upon a location of any large items that will be fitted underneath the worktop, such as a fridge. Don't worry about cupboards and storage – these issues will be tackled later. If you are fitting a fridge, for example, position it in the desired place and note the space around it for storage.

2   Make sure other equipment in the camper van isn't obstructed by your worktop and anything underneath it, such as the fridge mentioned in the last step. If you have a rock-and-roll bed, extend it outwards and check it doesn't catch the fridge.

3   Measure up the space you have for the worktop and find a suitable sheet of metal or wood to fit – some DIY stores will cut large sheets of wood or metal to size. This sheet of aluminium chequer plate is ideal because it's relatively light, but rigid.

4   Trial fit the worktop in position and use blocks of wood to determine its exact position. Make sure the worktop isn't too high or too low, especially if you intend to stand up when using it. Check the fridge door will open and mark the floor with masking tape to show this.

5   Decide how to mount the worktop. The back of the front seat squab

TOOLBOX

- Electric drill with 4mm drill bit
- Pop rivet gun and rivets
- Hacksaw
- Tape-measure
- Marker pen

Difficulty level: 3/5
On your own? Yes
Time: 3 hours

Trial fit any large items that need to be positioned under the worktop, such as a fridge.

Make sure the large items from step 1 do not obstruct other equipment, such as the rock-and-roll bed when it's flat.

Using the space available, measure up and find a cheap and lightweight worktop. This is aluminium chequer plate.

Use wooden blocks to locate the worktop and see if it's a suitable height.

shown here can be used to support the worktop with a length of angled aluminium used to hook over it or to form a mounting bracket.

6 Look for any areas on the camper van's inner panels that can be used to mount the worktop. Use angled aluminium to form mounting brackets, which can be pop-riveted in position. When drilling mounting holes, avoid drilling through to the outside.

7 The front of the worktop cannot

be secured to the van, so it has to be supported with a series of legs. Measure up and cut lengths of wood to create a supporting structure, which can be fixed to the worktop.

8 A hinged panel can be added to the worktop to act as a small table for one of the rear seat passengers. In this case, the end of the aluminium chequer plate was cut off and two hinges fixed between the two panels.

9 The finished worktop looks amateurish, but can be made to look more professional by vinyl wrapping the top of it. Cheap vinyl can be found on eBay and is relatively straightforward to fit (*see* separate instructions on vinyl wrapping).

10 Edging trim, such as angled aluminium, can be used to tidy up the worktop and provide a surface to mount other items, such as cupboards and doors.

Using a length of angled aluminium, the worktop can be attached to the seat squab.

A mounting bracket made from angled aluminium can be pop-riveted to the inside of the camper van.

Use lengths of wood to support the front of the worktop.

The worktop can be modified with a hinged panel to act as a fold down table.

It may look cheap and cheerful, but the worktop can be improved by wrapping it in vinyl.

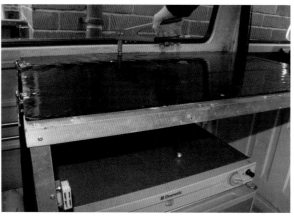

Here's the worktop being fitted again after it has been wrapped in gloss black and fitted with an angled aluminium edging strip.

CUPBOARDS

Storage is one of the most essential aspects of a camper van. Cutlery, pans, food and clothes are some of the items that need to be securely put away to ensure you can travel safely and use the van for eating and sleeping. Deciding where to build that storage can be difficult, along with what materials to use.

Most camper van interiors consist of an assortment of cupboards for storage and these can vary in size and quality of finish. Professional kits and materials look fantastic, but they can be expensive, and there's no harm in making your own from second-hand or cheap materials.

There are several issues to consider when planning and building cupboards to fit inside a camper van. The following points outline many of the common issues:-

◆ Bulky items: Think about what needs to go into the cupboards and where best to locate large items, such as a fridge, sink, hob and water tank. There may only be one or two places to put them, so you will have to build the cupboards around them.

◆ Beds and seats: Make sure the cupboards don't get in the way of sitting and sleeping inside the camper van. If you have a rock-and-roll bed, lay it down and, if the seats swivel, move them around before deciding where the cupboards can be fitted.

◆ Roof storage: There's usually lots of space around the roof area for additional storage, but make sure this won't restrict people from standing up and moving around. Lots of head-height cupboards can make an interior seem cramped and the additional top-heavy weight can affect the handling of the vehicle.

◆ Materials: Professional materials

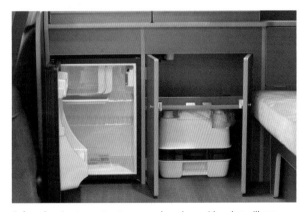

Before planning to construct some cupboards, consider what will go inside them.

Make sure equipment such as a rock-and-roll bed can be laid flat and won't be obstructed by the cupboards.

Cupboards in the roof provide useful storage, but can make an interior look cramped, and can affect head height and the vehicle's handling.

Professionally made kitchen kits are more expensive than a DIY build, but if looks are important, they are worth the expense.

Cupboard doors need to be securely kept shut. This pushbutton lock can be bought on eBay and through caravan parts' suppliers.

Kitchen-cupboard hinges provide flush-fitting doors, but require the right tools to fit them and 15mm-thick panels.

Bottom-hinged cupboard door with retaining straps is a cheap approach and ensures the contents inside cannot escape.

It looks awful when there's nothing inside this cupboard, but this wire mesh is easy to fit and is hidden when it's laden with food.

for making cupboards are expensive if you want to make sure it is lightweight, but cheap if you use general kitchen materials that are heavier. A professionally made set of cupboards and units will be more expensive than making them yourself, but they will probably have a better finish.

◆ Locks: Cupboard doors must be securely closed to reduce the risk of them opening when the camper van is travelling and objects spilling out – dangerous in the event of an accident. Pushbutton locks and similar components can be bought from caravan parts suppliers and eBay.

◆ Hinges: Household kitchen cupboard hinges are ideal for flush-fitting cupboard doors, but you will need to use a material for the doors that's at least 15mm thick. General metal hinges available from most DIY stores can be fitted to slimmer panels, but often don't look as professional.

◆ Alternative openings: There are many different ways of opening a cupboard, which enable cheaper

Don't be afraid to make a first attempt at some cupboards using scrap material to see if it works.

parts to be used and ensure the contents cannot escape so easily. A drawbridge style cupboard door, for instance, is one such example.

◆ Shelving: One of the less visible aspects of cupboards is its shelves, so these can often be constructed from cheap materials. Even light-weight wire mesh is useful, as it can be shaped to suit.

◆ Trial template: There's no harm in making some cupboards from scrap material to help test it and see if it really works. You can then remake the cupboard from better materials and possibly improve upon the design.

HOW TO MAKE KITCHEN CUPBOARDS

Kitchen cupboards don't need to be complicated, especially the structure behind the doors that will be filled with pans, cutlery and food. The following steps show how to create a very simple framework for a pair of cupboards that can be fitted beneath a worktop and around a fridge. Earlier in this chapter, there are ten steps showing how to build a simple and cheap worktop and the following steps assume the worktop has already been fitted.

The finish of the cupboards in the photographs that accompany the following steps may not be to everyone's taste and certainly look amateurish. However, the methods of constructing the cupboards provide the ideas for how you can create your own. Other materials can be used to achieve a completely different finish, and a lick of paint or roll of vinyl can produce some amazing results.

1 These steps assume a worktop has already been fitted and any objects that need to be fitted underneath it, such as a fridge, are already in position.

2 Horizontally hinged panels are useful for covering a gap between the top of a fridge and the worktop. Wood, aluminium sheet or a similar lightweight material can be used, fitted with hinges and wrapped in vinyl.

3 The hinged panel fitted in the last step can be locked using magnets that stick to the hinges, which are positioned on the vertical struts that support the kitchen worktop. There are other methods of locking the panel (*see* previous section).

4 A lightweight kitchen cupboard handle can be fitted to the front of the panel. Measure its position, drill

the mounting holes and fit retaining screws from the rear.

5 The top of the fridge can be used as a shelf, but there's usually a gap/drop at the back. A simple framework consisting of two lengths of wood for the sides and a sheet of metal can help.

6 If there's a large gap next to the fridge, it can house a shelf. First, a length of wood needs to be fitted next to the fridge to support the

Cupboards can be fitted underneath a worktop, using it as a framework to mount hinges for doors.

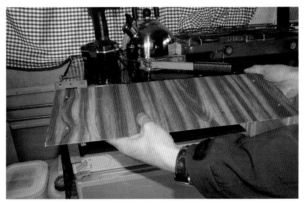

The space between the top of the fridge and the underneath of the worktop can be covered with a hinged panel.

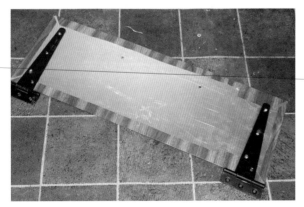

The hinges can be fitted on the back of the panel to hide them.

The front of the panel can be vinyl wrapped or painted.

Magnetic latches can be used to lock the panel in position.

A lightweight door handle from a kitchen cupboard is straightforward to fit on the outside of the panel.

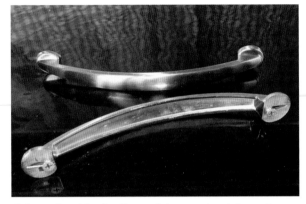

Kitchen cupboard door handles usually have two threaded mounting holes on the back.

The top of the fridge can be used as a shelf, but there's a gap at the back, which can be covered with this framework and a sheet of metal.

The framework and sheet of metal slides into position.

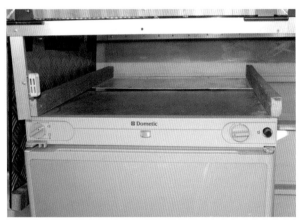

The top of the fridge can now be used as a shelf.

A vertical support fitted to the right of the fridge helps to secure the framework and the worktop.

The cupboard door will be mounted on the seat squab, but a straight piece of wood reveals it isn't straight.

worktop and act as a mount for the shelf. This can be attached to the framework from the last step.

7 The cupboard door that will cover the shelf requires a vertical panel to secure its hinges. The wood fitted in the last step can be used, or a new length fitted and secured to the inside of the camper van for instance.

8 Measure the available space inside the cupboard and look for a mounting point for a shelf. The inside of the camper van may have some ledges and strengthening beams, as shown in our photographs.

9 A shelf could consist of a flat panel, but a lighter option is to make a framework and cover it in a thin material. The framework can be as simple as four lengths of wood screwed together.

10 The shelf's framework can be secured to the vertical lengths of wood fitted in steps 6 and 7. At the back, the framework can sit on the metal ledges that are part of the inside of the camper van. Otherwise, mounting brackets would need to be fitted.

11 A light shelf can be fitted onto the framework. This could consist of a thin sheet of plywood or even wire mesh, folded and moulded to the shape of the shelf with a front lip and sides to stop objects falling out.

12 The shelf can be secured to the framework with a few screws. In the case of the wire mesh, large washers and screws are required to secure it to the framework.

13 The wooden framework has the advantage of being able to mount other items to it, such as hooks for mugs and utensils.

14 The bottom of the cupboard won't have anything inside to keep objects secure. The simplest solution is a collapsible box, which can be fed in when folded, then expanded to its full size.

15 Measure up the size of the hole for the cupboard door to cover, then cut out a sheet of wood or source some sheet metal. Fit two hinges

Screwing the wood to the seat squab ensures there's a straight edge to mount the cupboard door.

Before the cupboard door is fitted, measure inside to make a shelf.

This framework is being constructed to make a cheap and lightweight shelf.

The framework for the shelf can be screwed to the two vertical lengths of wood and can rest on a ledge at the rear.

Wire mesh is lightweight, easy to shape and useful for making a shelf.

The wire mesh can be loosely shaped with a front lip to prevent objects falling out, then easily manoeuvred into position.

Fit a few screws with large washers to secure the wire mesh in position.

Hooks can be fitted to the framework to hang mugs and utensils.

The bottom of the cupboard is bare, but a collapsible box can be manoeuvred inside.

Once it's opened up, the collapsible box cannot move, making it ideal for storing bulky items such as pans, a kettle and cereals.

Measure the required dimensions for the cupboard door.

The door can be made from thin wood or lightweight sheet metal like this one, which is being vinyl wrapped.

Double-check the dimensions of the cupboard door are correct before fitting it.

Loosely fit the top and bottom hinges of the cupboard door with a couple of screws, making sure it sits straight.

When you are satisfied the door is sitting straight, fit the remaining screws for the hinges.

Use a magnet and piece of metal to keep the cupboard door closed.

Mount the magnetic latch on a bracket, if it cannot be directly fitted in position.

down one side and, if required, paint the exterior or wrap it in vinyl.

16 Secure the door's hinges to the piece of wood fitted in step 7. Fit one screw through the top hinge, then secure the door so that it looks straight before fitting one screw through the bottom hinge. Fit all remaining screws.

17 Fit a magnetic latch onto the vertical length of wood next to the fridge and a piece of metal onto the door to ensure the two objects meet. This will be used to keep the door closed, but other methods of locking are outlined in the previous section and covered later in this chapter.

18 Lightweight kitchen cupboard door handles can be fitted onto the exterior of the door. In most cases, a couple of holes need to be drilled through the door to fit the retaining screws.

OVERHEAD LOCKER

Overhead lockers are a popular form of storage in a camper van, but they can be dangerous if they are not designed and fitted correctly. They must be securely fitted to a structural part of the camper van, such as a roof beam. The doors must be securely locked, with no risk of them flying open in the event of heavy braking. It is not advisable to make your own overhead locker unless you have the necessary skills and knowledge. Even if you buy a professionally made overhead locker, make sure you know how to fit it securely inside the camper van.

HOW TO FIT A SINGLE-LEG TABLE

A single-leg table kit is a neat and compact solution for including a table inside a van. The single leg cuts down on weight and allows cupboards and fridges to be opened, and the table is often wide enough for four people to squeeze around it.

Most single-leg tables consist of a sheet of wood for the table, a hollow metal pole for the leg and two metal cups for connecting the leg between the bottom of the table and the floor of the camper van. All of these parts can be bought separately or as a kit from most camper van and caravan specialists.

The work involved in fitting most single-leg tables includes drilling a hole in the floor, fitting a recessed base for the table leg and then constructing the table.

TOOLBOX

- Hole-cutter
- 6mm drill bit
- Electric drill
- Pencil
- Scissors or sharp knife
- Screwdriver
- Six long M6 bolts and nuts to secure base to floor
- Six short screws to fit to underside of table

Difficulty level: 2/5
On your own? Yes
Time: 2 hours

Drilling through the floor in a van can be dangerous. Make sure there are no obstructions underneath the floor where you are drilling. Check for brake and fuel pipes, and don't drill through a chassis rail. The base for the table leg sits inside a hole in the floor and protrudes through the bottom, so make sure there's nothing in the way before drilling.

Drilling a large hole in the floor requires the use of a hole-cutter, usually around 60mm in diameter.

Hole-cutters are available from most tool stockists, including Machine Mart. Be careful when drilling through a ribbed floor; the hole-cutter will grab and twist the drill at first, which can cause injury to your wrists and hands.

1 Remove everything from the floor area where the table will be secured. Trial fit the table to make sure everyone can sit around it. When everyone has agreed on a position for the table, mark the floor where the leg will stand.

2 Check what's underneath the floor where the table's mount will be fitted. If there are fuel or brake pipes, move them out of the way or choose another location. Similarly, if there is a chassis rail, find another location.

3 Use a suitable sized hole-cutter attached to a drill to cut the hole in the floor – check it's large enough to sink the aluminium base that will hold the table leg. Keep checking for obstructions underneath the floor when drilling.

4 Trial fit the table leg's base into the floor, making sure it doesn't foul anything underneath the floor. The base cannot be fully fitted until any

Trial fit the table to make sure everyone can sit around it.

Check underneath the floor before drilling the holes for the table leg's base.

carpets, vinyl or other floor coverings are refitted.

5 Refit any vinyl, matting or carpet, then cut through these with a sharp knife or scissors to allow the table leg's base to be fitted into the hole. Trial fit the base after the hole has been cut.

6 The table leg's base needs to be bolted through the floor. It usually has several holes, so use a suitable drill bit (e.g. 6mm) to drill through the floor covering and floor (check underneath the floor before drilling), then secure the base with some long bolts and suitable nuts.

7 Turn the table top upside down and use a tape-measure to find the centre. Trial fit the other base in the centre of the table, then use a pencil to mark the six holes. Also, draw around the base to help check it's correctly located.

8 Find six screws that are just long enough to secure the base to the table, but not too long that they will cut all the way through the table. Secure the base to the underside of the table with the screws.

9 Fit the table leg into the aluminium base in the floor, then fit the table on top of it. The leg is usually a tight fit in the base attached to the table and may need a little twist to remove it.

Use a hole-cutter to drill the hole for the base.

Trial fit the base, making sure it is a good fit.

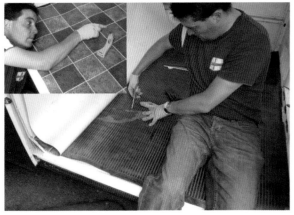
Cut the flooring to mount the table leg's base on top.

Drill holes through the flooring and floor to mount the table leg's base.

Secure the table leg's base with nuts and bolts.

Find the centre of the table to fit the mount for the table leg.

Secure the mount to the underside of the table with screws.

Here's the table installed in the camper van.

KITCHEN PODS

Self-contained kitchen pods are one of the best solutions for catering in a camper van. Professional kitchen pods can include all the essentials, such as a sink, cooker and room for a fridge. There are a number of manufacturers of kitchen pods, each with their own styling and methods of construction. If you are looking for a ready-made kitchen pod, decide what you really need and what you can do without. Space is limited when there is a fridge, cooker and sink with fresh- and waste-water tanks.

Kitchen pods can be manufactured from a variety of materials. The more expensive units use lightweight wood, such as Vohringer plywood that helps to keep the overall weight of the kitchen pod low.

Some kitchen pods are removable, making them ideal for outside catering, as well as routine interior maintenance. However, you may find they are too heavy to lift out on your own, especially if they are packed with food, crockery and pans.

Whilst the professionally made kitchen pods provide one solution to catering inside a camper van, a cheaper but more time-consuming option is to make your own. This isn't as easy as it sounds. Even if you rescue a set of kitchen cupboards from a house and make them fit, there's a lot of work involved in adding equipment such as a sink, cooker and fridge. Plus, kitchen units from a house are heavy, as they are usually made from chipboard, MDF and, in some cases, solid wood.

A kitchen pod doesn't necessarily need to be too sophisticated and in some cases, a compact unit is ideal, which houses some essentials for camping, leaving space inside the camper van for other equipment. So if you are looking at buying or making a kitchen pod, try to restrict what you need and keep everything as simple as possible.

Another important aspect of kitchen pods concerns styling. Many units that are available are very clean-looking

This kitchen pod from Bristol Transporters is made with lightweight materials and can be removed from the van for outside catering.

This full-width kitchen unit is neatly finished and looks relatively straightforward to construct, but will probably take most people several days to build.

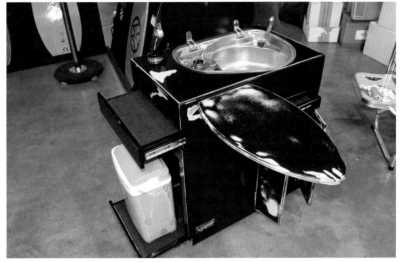

This retro-looking, compact kitchen pod from SC Campers has everything you need for cooking, washing and eating.

There are a number of ways to build a kitchen pod. If the panels you intend to use are strong enough, they can be used as the framework. If, however, you intend to use a light material, such as plywood or hardboard, to cover the sides, back and top of a kitchen pod, then in most cases, a framework should be constructed. The following steps reveal what's involved.

TOOLBOX

- Clamps
- Marker pen
- Saw
- Screwdriver
- Set-square
- Tape-measure

Difficulty level: 3/5
On your own? Easier with a second pair of hands
Time: 5 hours

---

with modern finishes. If you have a classic camper van, such a unit probably wouldn't look in keeping with the rest of the vehicle. There are, however, some manufacturers of retro-kitchen pods and it's worthwhile speaking to several suppliers to see if they can provide a more suitable finish.

If you cannot find a kitchen pod that fits your exact specification, there are plenty of camper van specialists who can build a bespoke unit for you. This isn't a cheap solution, but you will at least have something that features everything you need.

At the opposite end of the price scale, the cheapest solution to fitting a kitchen pod inside a camper van is to make one yourself. This is extremely time-consuming, but well worth the effort, especially if you can involve friends and family. The following pages cover a comprehensive guide to making a full-width kitchen pod, starting

with how to build the framework, followed by fitting shelves, cupboard doors and a worktop.

HOW TO BUILD THE FRAMEWORK FOR A KITCHEN POD

1   Before you embark on making a framework, position all the large items inside the camper van that will be fitted inside the kitchen pod or next to it. This will help to see the required dimensions of the pod.

2   Use a length of wood to determine the height of the framework. Remember a worktop will be fitted on top of it, so this isn't the overall height. Position the wood in different places to see if it's a suitable height.

3   When you have decided a height for the framework, cut several lengths of wood to make up the vertical sections (legs), which will be used to create the framework and allow shelves and cupboard walls to be fitted. Rough sawn 2 × 1½in wood is very cheap to buy and suitably strong.

4   Position the lengths of wood cut in the last step inside the camper van. Secure them with clamps to ensure they don't fall over. You can now

see the structure of the framework emerging.

5   The vertical lengths of wood can be joined with a long horizontal length of wood. First, cut a piece to length and place it on top of the vertical lengths that are positioned at the back of the kitchen pod.

6   Determine the position of each vertical length and mark them on the horizontal piece. You may want to fit the horizontal length of wood on top of the vertical sections, or

Fit all of the large pieces of equipment to see how the framework needs to be constructed. In this case, it will be built around both sides of the fridge.

Cut a length of wood to the desired height of the framework and test it in different areas.

Cut several legs for the framework, which will be used as the main structure and for fitting shelves and cupboard walls.

Trial fit the legs to see where the walls of the cupboards will be fitted and to help determine the structure of the overall framework.

Cut a length of wood to form the rear horizontal section of the framework. Mark the position of the legs.

Fitting the tops of the legs to the back of the horizontal length of wood may be easier than mounting it on top of the legs.

Secure the rear legs to the horizontal length of wood for the back of the framework.

Use screws or mounting brackets to attach the legs to the horizontal length of wood that forms the rear of the framework.

If your camper van is sitting level, then a spirit-level will help to ensure the framework is also level. Otherwise, check by looking at it.

Start at one end of the framework, preferably where there is some interior to align it to and clamp some wood in position.

Build the framework up gradually with a length of wood at one end that connects the rear leg with a front leg.

L-shaped brackets can help with securing pieces of wood together when making the framework.

fix them to the side. Decide which method is going to be easier and clamp the wood in position to test the structure.

7   Fix the vertical lengths of wood to the horizontal length. Use screws or mounting brackets. The resulting structure won't be rigid, so it's easy to adjust the legs. This forms the rear of the framework.

8   If you are confident that your camper van is sitting perfectly level, then try checking the positioning of the framework with a spirit level.

Otherwise, a visual check of the framework will have to do.

9   With the rear of the framework constructed, you can now start at one end and build it up. Assuming your camper van is not sitting level, the best method is to make sure each new piece of framework is fitted square to the existing structure and the surrounding panels in the camper van.

10 Starting at a side that has some interior of the camper van to line up to, cut a length of wood for the

side of the framework and assemble this with one of the legs cut in step 3. Secure the wood with screws and/or brackets.

11 Cut a length of wood similar to the horizontal rear section fitted in steps 5–8. This will form the front top section, so clamp some vertical lengths (legs) to it that were cut in step 3. Measure the rear section to find out exactly where they should be fitted.

12 Check the framework and resulting kitchen pod won't obstruct any-

thing, such as a sliding door handle. If it does, you may find the front horizontal length of wood cut in the last step needs to be shorter than the horizontal length at the rear.

13 Secure the front legs to the front horizontal length of wood and then fix this entire front assembly in position. You may have to use L-shaped brackets to fix the framework together.

14 The legs and horizontal length of wood at the front of the framework need to be flush (level) to be able to mount panels and cupboards. If the tops of the legs are mounted to the back of the horizontal length of wood, measure and cut a shorter leg to fit to the front of it.

15 The basic framework will still be very flimsy, but it can easily be made more rigid with some shelves. Before cutting a length of wood to fit and mount a shelf, make sure the corners of the framework are square.

16 Clamp a length of wood to a front and rear leg and use a tape-measure to make sure the distance from it to the top of the frame is the same on both legs. This piece of wood will form one mount for a shelf.

17 Cut two pieces of wood from the last step to length and fix them to the front and rear legs to form mounts for a shelf. Continue fitting more mounts for shelving, making sure the framework is square and the mounts are correctly measured.

18 The final piece of framework needs to support the top of the kitchen unit. Measure and cut two or three lengths of wood to fit between the front and rear horizontal lengths of wood.

Measure the distance between each leg at the rear to make sure the front legs are fitted to the same dimensions.

Clamp the front legs to a second length of wood to form the front of the framework.

Make sure the framework won't obstruct opening a door. If so, the framework will need to be altered.

The framework near the sliding door shown here needs to be shorter at the front and angled at the side to ensure there's access to the door's handle.

Secure the front framework (legs and horizontal length of wood) to the rest of the framework.

L-shaped brackets are often easier to fit than screwing two pieces of wood together.

The front of the framework needs to be flush to ensure cupboards and panelling can be fitted to it. The leg on the right isn't flush, so a second leg needs to be measured and fitted in front of it.

Fitting a second leg to the front legs strengthens them and ensures they are flush.

The framework will still be flimsy, so use a set-square to make sure the corners have 90-degree angles.

Clamp a length of wood to a front and rear leg and measure down from the top to ensure it's level. This will form a mount for a shelf.

The two lengths of wood fitted between the front and rear legs can be used to mount a shelf.

This angled side of the kitchen unit can still be equipped with shelves.

Measure some lengths of wood to fit between the front and rear horizontal sections of the framework across the top of the framework. This will help to support a worktop.

Use brackets and screws to fit lengths of wood that will act as supports for the kitchen pod's worktop.

HOW TO MAKE CUPBOARDS INSIDE A KITCHEN POD

Once a framework has been created for a kitchen pod, it will probably be quite flimsy, but can be strengthened with some thin panels that may not seem very strong, but once they are all fitted, the entire structure will be more rigid.

The panels that need to be fitted to the framework make up the floors and sides of the cupboards and they will be hidden by the cupboard doors and worktop, so their finish isn't particularly important. Even when they are seen from inside the cupboards, they will be largely concealed by food, plates and pans.

One of the best materials for lining the walls of cupboards is hardboard. It can be cut with a knife or pair of scissors, is lightweight and can be secured with small screws, nails or, in some cases, staples from a staple gun (providing the framework the staples are fitted to is sufficiently soft).

Hardboard isn't usually strong enough for the floor of a cupboard, unless you use two sheets. Instead, 6mm thick plywood is better and can easily be cut using a wood-saw.

Fitting the panelling for cupboards can be time-consuming. Make sure the framework is square before fitting a panel and use clamps to hold it in position whilst you secure it. If you are new to this type of work, don't get frustrated with gaps around the edges. These can be covered with trim or decorator's cork.

TOOLBOX

- Clamps
- Knife for cutting hardboard
- Marker pen
- Saw
- Scissors
- Screwdriver
- Set-square
- Tape-measure

Difficulty level: 2/5
On your own? Yes
Time: 6 hours

IT'S NOT SQUARE!

You may find that after removing the framework from your camper van, which you have created for the kitchen pod, it looks very flimsy and out of alignment. The panels inside the camper van may not be perfectly straight, so it's essential to build the kitchen pod inside to ensure it looks as straight as possible when fitted.

Thin hardboard can be cut with a knife or a large pair of scissors.

1 Source some suitable material to use for the walls of the cupboards. If the exterior of a wall isn't visible, then use hardboard, which can be cut with a knife. Otherwise, use 3–6mm thick plywood.

2 Starting with a cupboard wall, measure its width and height, making sure the framework is sitting square – use a set-square to check the corners of the framework are 90 degrees.

3 Cut a piece of hardboard or plywood to size and see if it can be fitted to form a cupboard wall. You may find it needs to be trimmed in places to fit flush.

4 When you are satisfied the panel fits flush, secure it with small screws, nails or, if the wood of the framework is soft enough, staples from a staple gun (only applies to hardboard).

5 Continue measuring, cutting, fitting and trimming the remaining walls of the cupboards. Look for locations on the framework where the walls can be secured.

6 The floor/shelf of a cupboard should be constructed from 6mm thick plywood or a similarly strong material. If you have some offcuts that are not large enough to make a shelf, you may find you need to fit two or more panels.

7 If you want to maximize the space inside a cupboard, the hardboard walls will need to be fitted on the outside of the framework and the plywood shelf will need to be trimmed at the corners to avoid the framework.

This piece of plywood was fitted to the back of a dresser and is ideal for making cupboard walls.

Hardboard is also useful for cupboard walls and can be cut with a knife.

Measure the dimensions of each wall and make sure the framework is square.

Slide the panel into position, making sure there are points on the framework where it can be secured.

This panel can move further upwards if its top corner is trimmed.

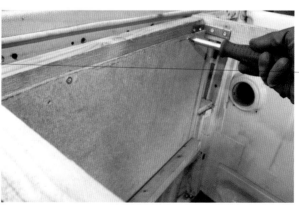
Hardboard walls can be secured with small screws to the framework.

If the framework's wood is soft enough, the hardboard panels can be secured with staples from a staple gun.

The back wall of the cupboard shown here won't be visible, so hardboard is ideal.

Cutting a notch out of the top corner of this panel helps to fit it flush.

Offcuts of plywood are ideal for shelves, but you may need a couple of panels if they aren't large enough.

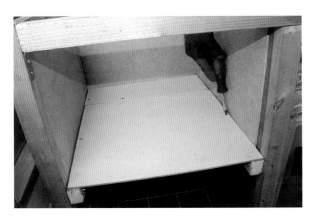

Secure the shelves to the framework with small screws.

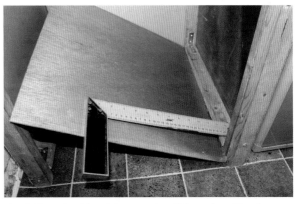

This shelf panel is wide and deep enough to fill the cupboard, but the corners need to be trimmed to avoid the framework.

After trimming the corners the shelf panel fits. It's not perfect, but a coat of paint and some decorator's cork around the edges will improve the finish.

This cupboard side will be visible from the outside as it's next to the fridge, so plywood is being used here for a better finish, which will be painted.

8   Any cupboard sides that are visible from the outside can be lined with plywood. Measure the size required, cut the plywood to shape and secure it with clamps.

9   The back of the kitchen pod probably won't be visible from the outside, so it can be covered over with a sheet of hardboard and secured with screws or panel pins (small nails).

10 If required, paint the framework, panelling and shelves. Bare wood should be painted with a primer first, followed by an undercoat and gloss or a one coat paint. After painting, fill any gaps with decorator's cork.

The back of the kitchen pod won't be visible from the outside, so it can be covered in a sheet of hardboard.

Use a roller to paint the kitchen pod's panels and frame. This produces a smoother finish.

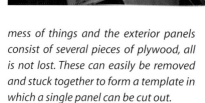

TOOLBOX

- Clamps
- Marker pen
- Saw
- Screwdriver
- Tape-measure

Difficulty level: 2/5
On your own? Yes
Time: 3 hours

HOW TO FIT EXTERIOR PANELLING TO A KITCHEN POD

The exterior panelling for a kitchen pod can take a lot of time to figure out and fit. The results need to be good, otherwise all the hard work that has been put into making the framework and fitting the cupboards will have been wasted. There is also less room for mistakes, unlike the shelves that will be covered with food, pans and other camping equipment.

Cutting the exterior panels can be disastrous if edges are not straight or if they are rough and chipped. Check your measurements before cutting and use a saw with small teeth that won't damage the wood. If you are confident using a jigsaw and can cut straight lines, then this will save time.

Expect to make a few mistakes when cutting the exterior panels, so it's often best to use a cheap material, such as plywood or MDF. If you make a complete

mess of things and the exterior panels consist of several pieces of plywood, all is not lost. These can easily be removed and stuck together to form a template in which a single panel can be cut out.

The following four steps show what's involved in the first stage of creating the exterior panels for a kitchen pod. The next section deals with making cupboard doors from them.

1   Measure and cut the panels to size that will be fixed to the exterior of the kitchen pod. Plywood is one of the lightest and cheapest materials to use. You may find you have several offcuts, so try clamping them in position to see how best to cut and fit them.

2   With the panels clamped in position, make sure they are not obstructing the opening of the fridge door, or concealing something that should not be hidden, such as a fire-extinguisher.

3   If any panels overlap, decide where to trim them to achieve the best finish. This can be difficult and you may find you have several panels to fit. Alternatively, you may want to create a template first, then cut it out of one large sheet of plywood.

4   Check the gaps and angles of the panels. You may find the floor of the camper van isn't straight, so the panels may need to be altered and trimmed along the top edge. This can take a lot of time.

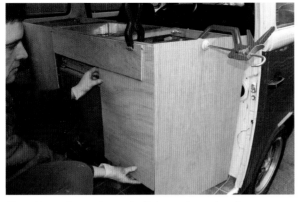

Clamp the exterior panels onto the kitchen pod to see how they can be fitted.

Make sure the door for the fridge isn't obstructed by the panels.

If panels overlap, decide the best way to cut them so they fit flush to the framework.

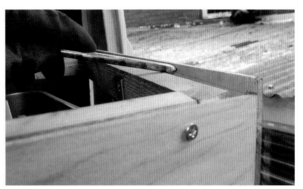

Make sure the panels look straight, even if the floor of the camper van probably won't be. Consequently, the top edges may need to be trimmed.

HOW TO MAKE CUPBOARD DOORS

Cutting out holes for cupboard doors can be a disastrous experience with the risk of wonky edges, but there are a number of ways to conceal those mistakes and produce a professional finish.

If you want to produce a kitchen pod with several cupboard doors that fit flush to their exterior panels and have concealed hinges with pushbutton locks, then be prepared to spend a lot of time carefully measuring, cutting, fitting and adjusting each door. The following steps show how to do this using cheap materials and DIY tools.

TOOLBOX

- Electric drill with 3mm drill bit
- Jigsaw
- Saw
- Screwdriver
- Tape-measure

Difficulty level: 4/5
On your own? Yes
Time: From 3 hours

---

1 Cutting out a hole for a cupboard door that's in the middle of a panel isn't easy. After marking the hole with a pencil and ruler, one method is to drill several small holes (3mm) to be able to slide a jigsaw blade in, then cut out the shape.

2 The edges of a hole are difficult to cut round with a jigsaw, so drill more holes before using the jigsaw again. This can be very difficult, especially if you want even round edges at all four corners.

3 If a cupboard door can be cut by starting at an edge of a panel, then it is much easier. Use a saw with small teeth to ensure a clean cut and make sure the edges are kept straight when cutting.

4 Another method of cutting out cupboards in the middle of a panel is to use a small saw and carefully

A jigsaw can quickly cut out a hole for a cupboard in the middle of a panel, but a steady hand is essential.

Drill small holes to cut around edges before continuing with the jigsaw.

The bottom of this panel will provide access to a cupboard, so the door can be cut up to the edge.

A cleaner way of cutting holes in the middle of a panel is to use small saw and cut across the surface of the panel. Use a straight edge for guidance and let the saw cut a groove.

Once a groove has been cut, keep cutting and eventually the saw will go all the way through the panel.

This adjustable hole saw can cut a round hole in a panel.

This side-mounted hinge can be secured to a piece of wood, which will be fixed to the kitchen pod's framework.

These bottom-mounted hinges are secured to a length of wood that will sit on the floor and be secured to the underside of a shelf.

cut across the panel. Use a straight edge to guide you and carefully let the front of the saw carve a groove through the wood.

5 Small, round holes can be cut in the middle of panels using a hole-saw. This is suitable for access holes, but not so good for holes where large objects need to be stored and retrieved.

6 Try to mount the hinges for the cupboard door on the kitchen pod's framework or on a length of wood that's thicker than the exterior panelling. This will make it sturdier and less likely to move or flex.

7 If a hinge has to be mounted onto an exterior panel, you may need to fit a piece of wood behind it for additional strengthening, unless the panel is sufficiently sturdy. This also applies to mounting the hinge onto the panel for the door.

8 Working out how to mount the hinges and whether the door can be opened is often very difficult, especially if you want the hinges to be concealed and the door to fit flush. It's easier to fit a door that overlaps and doesn't fit flush.

9 If you want to fit a door that closes neatly and fits flush, then one method is to carefully cut the door out of the panel, then fit the hinges on the outside. The hinges will be visible unless you use 15mm thick panels and kitchen door hinges.

Mounting a hinge onto this 6mm thick plywood panel may not be sufficiently sturdy, so fit a piece of wood behind.

The hinges for this door are fitted to two sheets of plywood to make sure the screws are long enough and don't go all the way through the layers of wood.

A door that overlaps its access hole is easier to fit than one that fits flush.

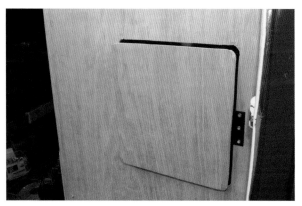

This door sits roughly half an inch away from the exterior panel, so the accuracy of its fitment isn't too important and trim can be fitted to hide any mistakes.

Exposed hinges need to be carefully measured and fitted to ensure they are evenly spaced.

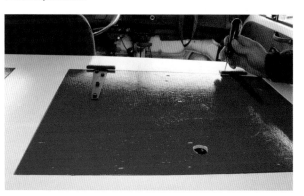

Flush-fitting doors with exterior hinges can have a good standard of finish and don't always cost a fortune.

HOW TO FIT LOCKS AND LATCHES TO CUPBOARD DOORS

There are a number of methods for locking a cupboard door to ensure it doesn't swing open and distribute tins, cereals and cutlery all over the floor. Magnetic catches and pushbutton locks as used by professional kitchen-unit manufacturers are quite straightforward to fit and the following steps show what's involved.

1 If a cupboard door overlaps, find and mark where a latch or lock can be fitted to the back of it. If possible, open the door slightly and mark the intended location of the lock or latch inside.

2 One of the simplest methods of securing a cupboard door is to use a magnetic catch and metal striker plate. Mount one or more magnetic catches around the opening for the cupboard.

3 The metal striker plate needs to be correctly positioned and the right shape to stick to the magnetic catch(es). Any steel plate can be used for this purpose, but it may need to be bent to shape to work properly.

4 A more professional-looking lock is a pushbutton-type. Most are intended to be fitted to 15mm-thick panels, but they can be modified. First, find where the lock should be fitted and measure the centre position across the width of the door.

5 Drill a 10mm hole where you want the pushbutton lock to be fitted. You should be able to then trial fit the lock and check the lock is in the correct position before drilling a larger hole in the next step.

6 Measure the largest diameter of the pushbutton lock (the round plastic collar in this case), then drill a hole to this size. If you don't have a suitable drill, use one that's smaller and enlarge it with a file.

7 Secure the pushbutton lock to the cupboard door with two screws.

The plastic collar may need to be cut down if it protrudes and it can also be glued in position.

8 An angled bracket may need to be fitted to make sure the lock's latch prevents the door from being opened. This can be fitted with two small screws. However, the edge of the panel can also be used for this purpose.

9 A finger hole is often sufficient to be able to open and close a door. Carefully measure its position to make sure it is central, then use a wood drill to make the hole. Clean up the cut with sandpaper and paint it, if necessary.

Open the door slightly and use a pencil to mark where a latch or lock can be fitted.

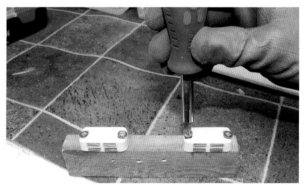

Magnetic catches can be mounted to a small piece of wood.

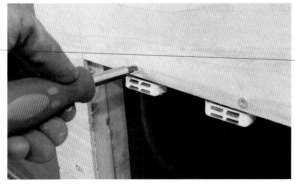

A piece of wood with magnetic catches fitted to it is easier to mount in position than trying to fit each catch.

Anything made from steel can be used as a striker plate for magnetic catches.

Measure and mark a location for a pushbutton lock, making sure it is central across the width of the door.

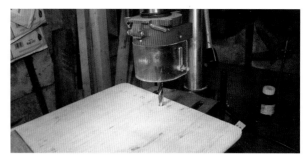

Drill a 10mm hole to allow the pushbutton lock to be trial fitted.

Test the lock to make sure the door can be closed and that it will lock and secure the door.

Measure the diameter of the plastic collar to see the size of hole that needs to be drilled.

If you don't have a large enough drill bit, enlarge the hole with a round or half round file.

Secure the lock to the back of the cupboard door with two small screws. Make sure they don't go all the way through the panel.

This pushbutton lock is designed for 15mm-thick panelling, but the door is 6mm thick, so the plastic collar can be cut down.

An angled piece of metal can be used as a catch to keep the door shut.

A finger hole can be drilled with a wood drill and is a cheap solution for opening a cupboard door.

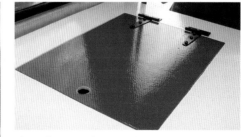

This worktop cover doesn't need any protruding handles or locks, so a finger hole is ideal.

HOW TO FIT A WORKTOP AND FINISH THE KITCHEN POD

The amount of work involved in making a kitchen pod can be more extensive than what is revealed in this book. There's no limit to the designs, equipment and accessories that can be fitted. Once the kitchen pod's framework has been constructed with cupboards fitted inside, the side panels cut and equipped with doors to the cupboards, the next stage is to paint the side panels, fit them, then start on the worktop. The following steps show what's involved.

TOOLBOX

- Jigsaw or saw
- Pencil
- Screwdriver
- Tape-measure

Difficulty level: 2/5
On your own? Yes
Time: From 3 hours

---

1. Start with a large sheet of plywood and place it on top of the kitchen pod. If it's too big, mark where it needs to be trimmed and decide whether you want it to overlap or fit flush to the side panels – an overlap is easier.

2. If you need to cut some holes in the worktop to access a stove or cupboards, then refit it and mark where these holes must be cut. Also, measure the dimensions of any required holes, especially the stove.

3. Mark the measurements for cutting out holes in the worktop. It may be difficult to check whether they are correct, so return to the kitchen pod and check them again.

4. There are a number of different ways to cut out holes in a worktop,

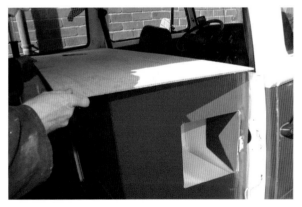

Trial fit the worktop to see where it needs to be trimmed.

Decide whether you want the worktop to fit flush to the sides of the kitchen pod or overlap.

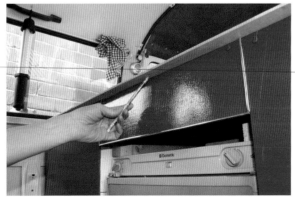

It can be difficult to mark where any holes need to be cut in the worktop, so use a pencil to mark around parts of the kitchen pod.

Lift the worktop and mark underneath to indicate where the hole should be cut for the stove.

Carefully measure and draw the position of any holes that need to be cut in the worktop.

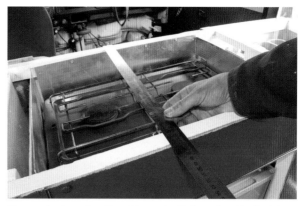

Measure the size and position of the required holes and double-check these against the markings on the worktop.

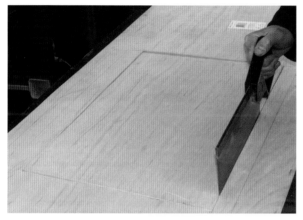

Cut out each hole in the worktop. Using a small saw to cut through the panel produces a neater finish than a jigsaw.

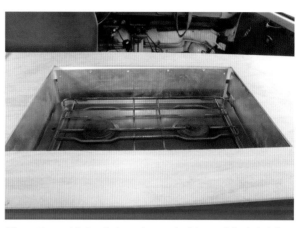

After cutting each hole, refit the worktop to check it, especially the hole for the stove.

Once all of the holes have been cut, it's time to decide on a colour for the worktop and apply it.

Apply a coat of primer to bare wood, then either undercoat and a top coat or a one coat finish.

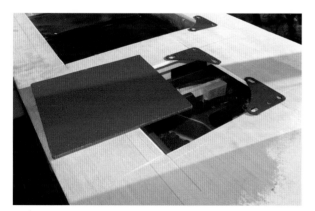

These metal brackets can be secured to the underside of the worktop to support the cupboard doors.

When the worktop is fitted, this is all you can see of the metal support brackets.

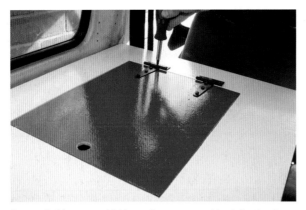

Secure all of the covers with hinges, then once everything is fitted and tested, secure the kitchen pod to the camper van.

Here's the completed kitchen pod, which has been made from three sheets of plywood, one sheet of hardboard, several lengths of 2×1 wood, a handful of hinges and locks and a small tin of paint. Total cost is under £100.

which were explained earlier in this chapter, including using a drill and jigsaw, a small saw and a hole-cutter.

5   After cutting each hole, refit the worktop to check it is correct. This is especially important for a stove, where the hole needs to be large enough to ensure the worktop won't be burned.

6   Once all the holes have been cut in the worktop, fit it back onto the kitchen pod for a final check before painting it. Start with a primer for bare wood, followed by a one coat gloss or undercoat and gloss.

7   The cupboard doors on the worktop need to be adequately supported so that objects can be placed on top of them. Secure wood or metal strips to the underside of the worktop to help support these opening panels.

8   Fitting hinges and locks was covered earlier in this chapter. Once all the covers have been equipped with these items, the final stage is to secure the worktop to the kitchen pod and secure the kitchen pod to the interior of the camper van.

HOW TO HIDE MISTAKES

Unless you are extremely lucky, very careful or highly skilled, then mistakes will be made when making a kitchen pod. In most cases, these mistakes can be rectified or concealed, and the following suggestions reveal some of the tricks of the trade.

◆   Plastic trim: Rough, uneven edges can be covered over with plastic

trim that's used for fitting bathroom or kitchen tiles. It can be cut with a sharp knife and secured using a strong glue.

◆   Chrome trim: Fitted to cars, this plastic, flexible, self-adhesive trim has a chrome finish and is perfect for sticking onto rough edges and hiding lines where panels

meet. It can be cut with a sharp knife and will stick to most surfaces.

◆   Rubber seals: Suitable for fitting around cupboard doors or holes that have been cut out. Seals can be found on cars in a scrapyard or at auto-jumbles, but check their internal measurements to ensure they

Rough and uneven edges around a cupboard opening can be concealed with plastic trim that's used for tiling. Cut it with a knife and glue it in position.

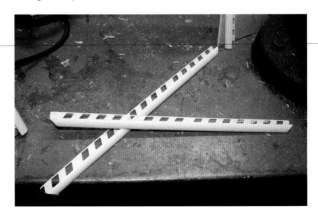

This plastic trim for tiling can be fitted between panels or along edges of panels.

can be fitted onto your kitchen pod's panels.

◆ Decorator's cork: Useful for filling panel gaps between shelf panels and cupboard sides. Available from most DIY stores and applied with a gun/cage. Can be smoothed and manipulated using a finger, then left to dry before being painted.

◆ Screw caps: The heads of screws may not look too ugly, but for a more professional finish, fit a plastic screw cap. Available from DIY shops and eBay.

◆ Round edges: Cut, sand and round off the corners of panels for a neater finish. Also, rub down the edges of panels to remove rough sections and fragments of wood.

Chrome trim for cars is available in a reel. It's flexible, self-adhesive, easy to cut and can hide panel gaps and rough edges.

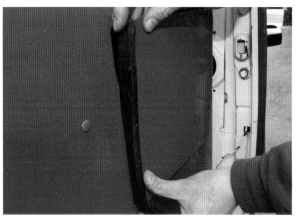

Rubber seals found on cars can help to hide uneven edges around cupboard doors.

Decorator's cork is useful for filling gaps and once dry, it can be painted.

Plastic screw caps help to cover any exposed screw heads.

Carefully cut and shape sharp corners to round them off, then sand them down.

Sand down all edges of panels for a smoother finish.

HOW TO MAKE A SINK

Camper van and caravan sinks can be expensive to buy along with many of the additional components including the pump, tap and water tanks. However, it is possible to make your own sink from a variety of readily available materials. Here are some examples of the types of components that can be used:

- *Dog bowl: A large stainless steel feeding bowl for dogs will cost less than £10 and can be used as a compact sink inside a camper van.*
- *Plug hole: Most DIY shops sell sink drainage and plug-hole kits with all the necessary seals and attachments.*

TOOLBOX

- Dot punch
- Electric drill with hole-cutter
- Gloves and goggles
- Round or half-round file
- Screwdriver
- Scribe
- Silicone sealant
- Straight edge or ruler

Difficulty level: 3/5
On your own? Yes
Time: From half a day

- *Shower head: An old shower head can be used for a tap, although plastic sink taps for caravans are not too expensive.*
- *Water container and pump: A plastic windscreen-washer container from a car can be used as a fresh-water container and many include an electric 12-volt pump that can run off the leisure battery. Make sure you thoroughly clean and sterilize inside the container, especially if you intend to drink the water.*
- *Waste water bottle: An old 5ltr plastic bottle can be used to collect waste water.*
- *Vacuum cleaner pipes: Vacuum cleaner pipes can be used to connect the sink drain to the waste water bottle. Drainage pipes for kitchens and bathrooms can also be used and are available from most DIY shops.*

A sink generates a new set of rules concerning hygiene and safety, especially if the water that comes from its tap is going to be used for drinking. The fresh-water tank, pipework, pump and tap all need to be thoroughly cleaned and sterilized prior to use and this must be repeated at least once a year. If the camper van or the sink is not used during winter, then everything must be dismantled and cleaned to reduce the risk of mould and bacteria. If this sort of maintenance puts you off, then consider using a sink for hand-washing, or having one without a tap where it can be used to wash dishes with hot water from the kettle.

If, however, you want to have fresh water flowing in your camper van, which can be used for drinking, then it's not advisable to use a windscreen-washer bottle from a car. Even if the bottle and pump are adequately cleaned and sterilized, most washer bottles cannot store enough water for drinking. Instead, use a dedicated water container for camping and buy a pump from a camping or caravan specialist.

There are a number of ways to build a sink, so the following steps outline some general ideas, showing how to use a feeding bowl and several other cheap and readily available items.

A new, large feeding bowl can be bought from a pet shop and used to make a sink.

Plug hole and drainage kits are available from DIY shops.

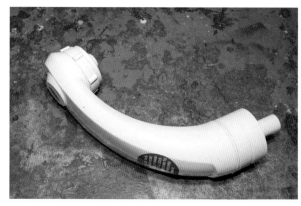

A cheaper solution to this plastic tap for caravan and camper van sinks is to use an old shower head or household tap.

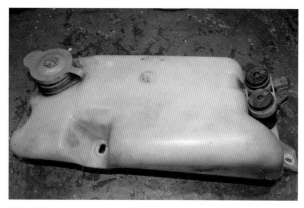

This windscreen-washer container and pump from a Rover Metro is cheap to buy from a breakers yard, but must be thoroughly sterilized.

A small 5-litre waste-water tank is sufficient for light use and is often free. This one is used to store windscreen-wash solution for cars.

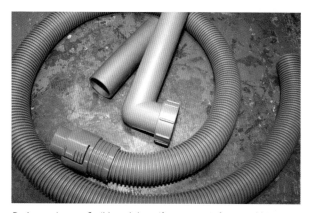

Drainage pipes are flexible and cheap if you use parts from an old vacuum cleaner.

1   Turn the feeding bowl upside down and find the centre of the base where the drain hole will be fitted. Use a ruler or straight edge to mark across the centre and eventually you will be able to measure or locate it, then mark it with a dot punch.

2   Look at the plug hole cover that will be fitted inside the sink on the base. Find a suitable hole-cutter that is the same size. This is the best way to cut a hole in the base of the feeding bowl. It is possible to cut a hole using a jigsaw, but this can be awkward and time-consuming.

3   Carefully cut out the hole in the base of the feeding bowl using the hole-cutter. Wear gloves to protect your hands and goggles to protect your eyes. This can be dangerous as the hole-cutter may get trapped when cutting and sharply twist the drill.

4   After cutting out the hole, file the edges to remove any rough bits of metal, then check the plug hole cover can be fitted. Continue filing if it's too tight. If a seal is supplied with the plug hole cover, make sure it can be fitted.

5   Assemble the plug hole cover with the drain attachment underneath. Use any seals supplied in the drain kit and apply sealant to help prevent leaks. Most kits include a screw that fits through the plug hole cover and is threaded into the drain attachment below.

6   With the feeding bowl converted into a sink, consider how the water inside it will be drained and collected. Flexible vacuum cleaner pipe could be used, or more rigid and conventional household drainage

Turn the feeding bowl upside down and locate the centre by measuring and scribing across it.

Find a hole-cutter that is large enough to cut out a hole in the base of the feeding bowl and locate the plug hole cover.

pipes and collected in a plastic bottle. Also, look at where the sink will be installed to see how much space you have.

7 There are various ways to fit a sink inside a camper van, depending on whether a kitchen unit already exists. If a new worktop needs to be made to fit the sink, use a material that can withstand being soaked. Position the sink upside down on the worktop, draw around it, then calculate a slightly smaller hole to cut, so the sink can be slotted in and supported.

8 A sink doesn't necessarily need to have a tap – warm water from the kettle can be used to wash the dishes. If you decide to fit a tap, there are a number of options. One of the cheapest is to buy a second-hand windscreen-washer bottle and electric pump from a car breakers yard and connect this with plastic tubing to a tap.

Carefully drill a hole in the base of the feeding bowl. Protect your hands and eyes with gloves and goggles.

Clean the edges of the hole with a round file to help remove any sharp metal fragments.

Fit the plug hole cover and securing screw, then thread it into the drain attachment underneath the feeding bowl.

This flexible vacuum-cleaner pipe can be used to drain and collect waste water from the sink.

A short, straight plastic pipe between the sink and a plastic waste-water bottle is compact and ideal for installing in a camper van kitchen.

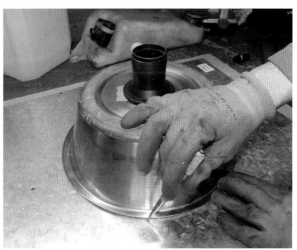

This metal sheet is from an old tumble dryer and can be used for the sink's surrounding worktop. Scribe around it as shown, then cut a smaller hole so the sink won't fall through when fitted.

This windscreen-washer bottle and motor from a Rover Metro can be powered via an inline fuse to the leisure battery. Plastic tubing can feed water from the pump to a tap.

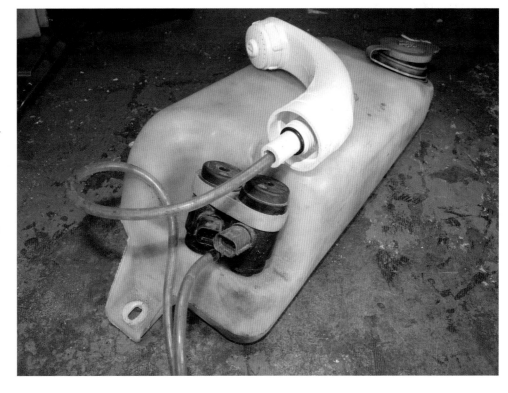

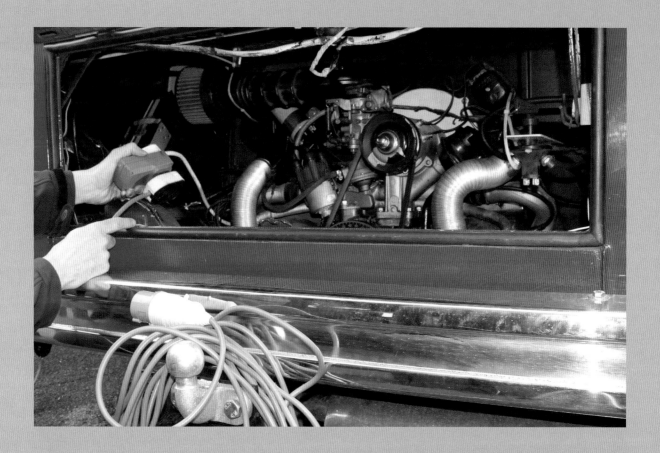

electrical equipment

A camper van requires electricity of some sort for lighting, operating a fridge and powering entertainment systems. This chapter outlines the different sources of electricity, how it can be supplied to a camper van and the type of equipment that can be used.

be used in a camper van, but with a few more luxuries, such as a permanent position for the power sockets and a connection underneath the camper van that leads inside, so you don't have to leave a door open with a lead trailing through.

Safety is very important when it comes to electricity, especially when you consider that mains electricity is rated at 240 volts. Many campsites have their own safety features to prevent surges of power, but it's wise to have your own in the form of circuit-breakers, surge protectors and

HOOKING-UP FOR ELECTRICITY

Anyone who has spent years camping without electricity usually never looks back when they invest in a hook-up. In the case of a camper van, it's essential if you want to power a fridge, television and lighting. There are of course, other solutions, but a main electricity power supply is straightforward and doesn't need to cost a fortune to connect to your camper van.

On a very basic level, which is similar to camping with a tent, a hook-up can consist of a cable with a two- or three-pin plug connection at one end for connecting to the campsite's electricity supply, and one or more sockets at the other end to power electrical equipment, such as a fridge. This setup can easily

Most campsites have a series of hook-up points where you can connect a special lead to be able to operate electrical equipment.

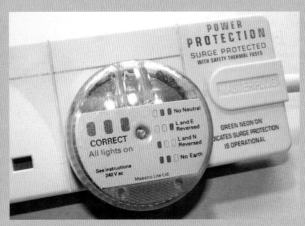

A socket tester can help to identify whether a campsite's electricity is wired differently to your camper van and potentially avoid any dangerous electric shocks.

fuses. Some household extension leads have these features built in and you can also buy RCD circuit-breakers that are used with electrical equipment such as hedge-trimmers and lawn-mowers.

It is also worthwhile carrying a socket tester in the camper van and running through a test of the supply after you have connected to the mains electricity at a campsite. This can help to identify any problems with the campsite's electricity, which may be wired differently. It's potentially more of a problem on European campsites where the live and neutral feeds are switched. Plugging in a socket tester should identify this problem and save you from any unwanted electric shocks – the metal parts of some electrical appliances may become live and will give you an electric shock if you touch them.

The following steps provide a cheap solution to using mains electricity in a camper van. This book does not cover the fitting of a professional system, which should be installed by a qualified electrician.

This lead has a three-pin plug, which can be used on the majority of UK campsites.

Some European campsites use a two-pin plug for electric hook-ups, so you may need to buy a converter.

This mobile mains supply unit from Pennine Leisure Supplies has a 20m cable and an RCD circuit-breaker.

A hook-up lead with one socket on the end can be extended, but take precautions and fit an RCD circuit-breaker.

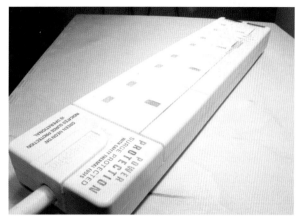

If you intend to use an extension, source one with safety features such as surge protection.

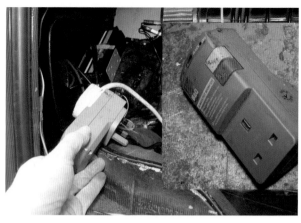

An RCD circuit-breaker can be bought from most DIY shops and can help protect your electrical appliances.

The hook-up connector can be mounted under the camper van, but must be kept dry.

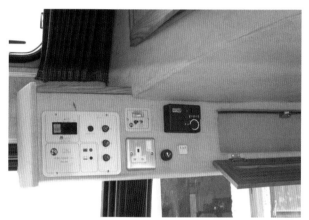

Professional equipment for controlling the electrical supply to the camper van includes fuses and battery monitors.

This setup uses a domestic consumer unit and is fitted with a short hook-up lead and socket that's accessed via a reflector panel in the bumper.

Connecting at a Campsite

1   UK campsites have a three-pin plug to provide electricity to your camper van. Invest in a long lead as you may not always be parked next to the electricity connection.

2   Many European campsites have a two-pin plug instead of a three-pin plug. Fortunately, adapters are available and are best bought before you travel.

3   One of the simplest ways to connect to mains electricity at a camp- site is to buy a kit with the right two/three-pin plug at one end and a bank of sockets at the other end to plug in and power electrical items.

4   If you have only one socket on the end of the hook-up lead, then an extension lead with multiple sockets can be used to connect to it. This has the benefit of being able to fix the extension lead permanently inside the camper van.

5   Make sure the equipment you use has a safety cut-off feature, such as an RCD circuit-breaker and surge protection, built into the extension lead. Some campsites have their own circuit-breakers, but have your own to be safe.

6   Permanent fixings, such as a hook-up connector can be fitted, if required. There are also electricity kits and equipment with fuse boxes and switches for main and leisure battery supply.

HOW TO FIT EXTRA POWER SOCKETS

Additional power sockets are useful in a camper van for ensuring a number of electrical items can be operated without having to overstretch their wires. The easiest and quickest solution is to fit an extension lead with additional sockets. Providing it has mounting holes, the extension lead's sockets can be secured to a surface with screws or bolts and the wiring can be tied down. However, if you are competent with household electrics and able to wire a plug, then a better solution is to fit electrical sockets. The following step-by-step guide shows how to mount electrical sockets inside a camper van and route cabling to them. Do not do this if you are unsure about electrics.

Make sure you purchase suitable cable for connecting an electrical socket and put safety at the top of the list. Use a socket with switches and, if possible, safety features such as a fuse. An RCD circuit-breaker should be included somewhere in the camper van's electrics, preferably between the main connection and

the lead that's connected to a campsite's electrics. Similarly, some form of surge protection must be used, which is incorporated into the more expensive extension leads.

After fitting sockets into a camper van, use a socket tester to make sure they are correctly wired and regularly check them – connect an electricity supply from your house using an extension reel. When visiting a campsite, always perform a test of the electrics using a socket tester to make sure the campsite's electrics are wired up in the same way as your camper van's electrics.

1   Trial fit the electrical socket inside the camper van and consider which electrical appliances will be connected to it. This will help to determine where it should be fitted.

2   Make sure all the electrical items you intend to connect to the socket

TOOLBOX

• Socket tester
• Insulated screwdriver
• Wire-cutters and strippers
• Electric drill and drill bits

Difficulty level: 3/5
On your own? Yes
Time: 1 hour

SAFETY REGULATIONS

In countries such as the UK, wiring and sockets that are powered by the mains electricity supply can only be fitted by a qualified electrician, or must be checked and tested by someone who is qualified.

can be fitted. Some plugs need more space as they are bulky, so the socket may need to be mounted on an angle or away from a window.

3   Work out how to mount the electrical socket and feed the wires through to it. Most have mounting holes at the back (unscrew the front cover), which may need cutting out if the base is made from plastic.

4   Once you have decided upon the location of the electrical socket, fit the base and make sure it is secure. It needs to be firmly located as plugs will be pushed into it and pulled out.

5   Using suitable cabling, connect the appropriate wires to the front panel of the electrical socket. The colours of the wires and where they should be fitted may vary, so do not use our illustrations as a reference.

6   Take the cable that is connected to the electrical socket and connect it to a power source. It can be equipped with a plug so that it can be plugged into a socket or fitted direct to a consumer unit.

The easiest way to include more electrical sockets inside a camper van is to use an extension lead.

7 Secure the cabling that's connected to the electrical socket, making sure it cannot get damaged, caught or stretched. Make sure there's a means of switching off and isolating the socket – a plug connection is ideal in this situation.

8 The socket needs to be tested. You probably won't be at a campsite, so use an extension reel to connect to the mains electricity in your house, then use a socket tester to check the wiring in the electrical socket is correctly connected. Test this frequently.

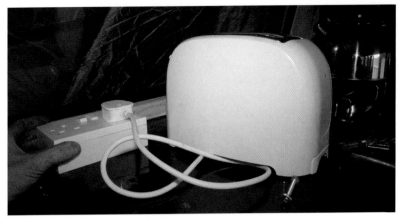

Fitting an extra socket on this worktop enables this toaster to be used without over stretching its cable.

This homemade mounting bracket allows the electrical socket to be mounted on an angle, but make sure a range of appliances can be connected to it.

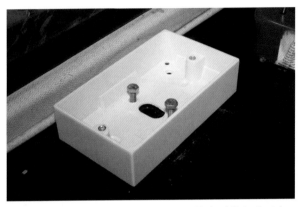

This socket base can be bolted to the worktop and holes drilled to feed the wires through the back of it.

Make sure the base of the electrical socket is secure. Plugs will be pushed and pulled against it.

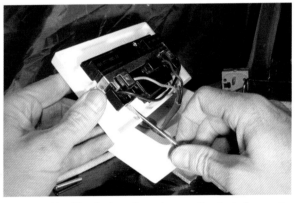

Source suitable cabling for the socket and connect the wires in the correct order. Do not do this unless you know what you are doing.

Connect the cable from the electrical socket to a power source. Here we have fitted a plug and connected it to one of the existing sockets in the camper van.

Secure the cable that's connected to the electrical socket, making sure it cannot be stretched or damaged.

Connect a power supply to the electrical socket to be able to test it.

Use a socket tester to make sure the electrical socket has been correctly wired.

HOW TO FIT A LEISURE BATTERY

A second battery is known as a leisure battery and can be used to provide power to internal lighting, a fridge and other electrical components associated with a camper van. Most leisure batteries are more substantial than a standard battery, which is used for the vehicle's engine and are usually rated at 90 or more amp hours, whereas a vehicle battery (used for starting the engine and providing power for headlights, the stereo and similar equipment) is often less, at between 50 and 70 amp hours. Consequently, most leisure batteries are much heavier than a standard battery.

A leisure battery is intended to supply power over a long period of time, whereas a standard car battery is designed to produce high power over a very short period of time for starting the engine, for instance. A leisure battery also has a greater ability to be discharged and recharged, which is called deep cycling.

Fitting a second battery requires a number of points to be addressed. The first involves determining a location for the battery, which is covered in this section. You also need to consider how the battery is going to be recharged and how the battery will provide power to electrical components inside the camper van. All of these points are covered over the next few pages.

There are a number of safety points to address when fitting a second battery. It's important to remember that a battery is a heavy object, so it must be securely fitted to make sure it doesn't become airborne in the event of heavy braking or an accident. Most batteries contain lead acid, which can leak out, especially if a battery is old, resulting in

corrosion. The acid is harmful to skin, so wear gloves when handling a battery. When manoeuvring and securing a battery, avoid touching both terminals with a metal object such as a spanner, and avoid earthing the positive terminal (e.g. touching it with a spanner that makes contact with the bodywork). Sparks may fly and cause injury.

Finally, the photographs in this section show the fitting of a battery to a vehicle with a negative earth, which is commonly found on modern vehicles. If your camper van is old and has a positive earth (i.e. the lead connected to the positive terminal on the engine's battery is connected to an earth point on the vehicle), then make sure you connect the terminals correctly and check that the leisure battery you intend to use as a second battery is suitable.

1　Find a suitable location for the second battery. Some camper vans have space under the front seats

designed specifically for storing a battery. Make sure there's room to store a battery and that it can easily be manoeuvred into position and removed.

2　The space shown in this rear engine bay on a VW Bay Window camper is suitable for fitting a second battery. A metal box has been fitted to store the battery, which has been pop riveted to the bodywork.

3　Making sure the battery can be isolated and switched off is a good

---

TOOLBOX

- Electric drill with 4–8mm drill bits

Difficulty level: 1/5
On your own? Yes
Time: 1 hour

idea to help preserve its voltage and reduce the risk of electrical fires. This battery cut-off switch can be fitted between the earth (negative on most) terminal and earth point on the vehicle.

4 The earth lead for the battery needs to be secured to a suitable earth point on the vehicle, such as the bodywork or a chassis leg. Drill a hole to fix the earth lead with a nut and bolt. Clean any paint off the surrounding hole, which may affect earthing.

5 Trial fit the battery in its location and fit the earth lead with its cut-off switch. Make sure the battery is securely fitted and the cut-off switch can be operated.

6 The battery must be securely located, with no risk of it moving or falling over during cornering or braking. If necessary, buy a universal clamp or strap from a car accessory shop to secure the battery (they can also be found on scrap cars at breakers yards).

USING THE POWER

There are a number of methods of connecting electrical components to a second battery. If components such as a fridge and lighting are powered by either the second battery or main electricity when a hook-up is attached at a campsite, then a specialist manufactured control unit can be used to either manually or automatically switch between the two. These are available from most camper van specialists, but you will probably be advised to have

Camper vans, such as this VW T25, have space for batteries under the front seats.

The metal box on the left can be used to house a second battery and has been pop-riveted to the body of the camper van.

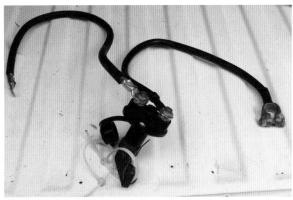

A battery cut-off switch is useful for switching off the supply from a second battery when it is not in use.

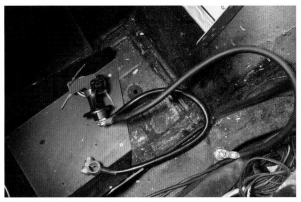

A good earth point is essential for a battery. Drill a hole through a metal panel and secure the earth lead with a nut and bolt.

Second battery and its cut-off switch fitted.

A battery clamp from a scrap car in a breakers yard can be used to secure a battery.

such equipment fitted by a professional for safety reasons. DIY approaches to powering a second battery are a little simpler. If a fridge can be powered by 12 volts or mains electricity, it may have a switch on it to choose the appropriate supply. Consequently, you should be able to connect suitable wiring from the battery to the fridge and also to an earth point. An inline fuse may be required and a minimum thickness of cabling to avoid overheating.

Other components, such as internal lighting, can be run directly from the battery, but will require some type of fuse or fuse box to ensure that in the event of an electrical problem, the fuse blows first instead of the wiring starting to melt and catch fire.

Inline fuses can be connected to each power lead that runs from the battery to equipment such as lighting or a fridge. Make sure the inline fuse is fitted close to the connection at the battery, so that if an electrical problem occurs, the fuse should blow and only the short length of wire to it can potentially be damaged.

Several inline fuses connected to the live terminal on the leisure battery can look messy. A better solution is to use a fuse box with one or several wires from the leisure battery connected to it. This allows all the fuses to be neatly located in one place.

There are a wide range of aftermarket fuse boxes available. The cheapest require separate live wires to be connected to each fuse, whereas more expensive fuse boxes have one live connection from the leisure battery. There are even fuse boxes with LED warning lights, which illuminate when a fuse has blown.

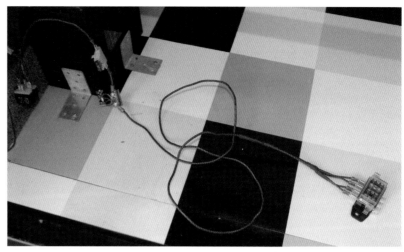

The fuse box on the right has four connections and takes the power from the live terminal on the leisure battery.

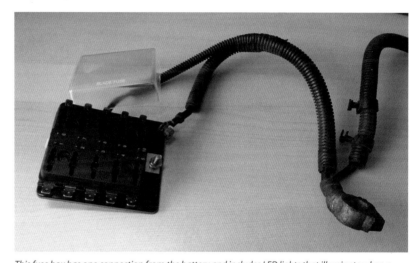

This fuse box has one connection from the battery and includes LED lights that illuminate when a fuse has blown.

A leisure battery can be used to operate electrical equipment that only uses 240 volts (i.e. mains electricity supply). The solution is to fit an inverter, which alters the 12 volts from the leisure battery and produces the same 240 volts supplied by mains electricity, so any mains-operated equipment can be connected directly.

Inverters are rated according to how many watts they produce and most won't produce enough power to operate a toaster or kettle. They are useful for operating a fridge, television and

An inverter converts a 12-volt supply from a battery into 240 volts, allowing mains operated equipment to be powered.

Most inverters are cooled via an internal fan, so they can be noisy.

lighting. However, there are a number of safety precautions you need to be aware of concerning using an inverter. The inverter produces 240 volts from a 12-volt battery and is often earthed to the battery. Many specialists advise using an additional earth into the ground, such as a metal spike, to avoid the danger of an electric shock when you touch the bodywork of the camper van. Second, inverters have a fan to help keep them cool. This can be noisy, but don't cover the inverter and risk it overheating. Also, don't fit an inverter next to the engine where it is warm, and most inverters should not be used when the engine is running.

Solar energy provides a small amount of electricity, which can be used to keep a battery topped up. This solar panel is from Just Kampers and helps to keep a battery topped up.

RECHARGING A SECOND BATTERY

A second battery, which is used to power camper van equipment such as a fridge, television and lighting, needs to be recharged to avoid becoming flat. There are a number of solutions available, which are listed below.

◆ Mains charger: One of the simplest methods of recharging a second battery is to connect it to a battery charger, but this requires the vehi-

A split-charge system uses power from the camper van's alternator or dynamo to recharge the leisure battery. This kit is available from Just Kampers.

Attaching a battery charger to a leisure battery can quickly recharge it, but requires mains electricity.

◆ Split charge: A number of wiring kits are available to allow the alternator or dynamo in a camper van to recharge a second battery, as well as the vehicle's battery. This is known as a split-charge system. The work involved in fitting this system is covered in the next section.

HOW TO FIT A SPLIT-CHARGE SYSTEM

A split-charge system enables a second battery (leisure battery) to be recharged by the camper van's alternator or dynamo. Leads are connected between the vehicle's battery and the leisure battery, with safety relays and controls to prevent problems arising.

If you are familiar with vehicle electronics, then the method of supplying charge to the second battery is quite straightforward. There are, however, some potential problems that can arise, so it is worthwhile purchasing a split-charge kit from a camper van or elec-

cle to be stationary and located where a mains electricity supply is available. It's a practical solution if you intend to use the leisure battery for a few hours, then return home or to a campsite where it can be recharged.

◆ Solar panel: Most solar panels can provide a trickle charge to help keep a battery topped up, but do not provide enough power to recharge a battery that is flat. This solution is only viable for long-term storage of the camper van. Solar panels are available from camping and electronics specialists.

tronics specialist. The following points outline some of the issues that need to be considered when choosing a suitable split-charge system.

- ◆ Engine running: Make sure the split-charge system only recharges the leisure battery when the engine is running. It must not be able to drain the power from the vehicle's own battery without the engine running, otherwise it will be flattened.
- ◆ Safety cut-off: If the leisure battery's voltage is too low, it may need to be recharged using a mains charger as it could be too much for the split-charge system. Make sure there is a fuse or relay switch in the split-charge system as a precaution.
- ◆ On/off charging: There must be some means of switching the charging of the leisure battery on and off. This may be when the engine is running via a relay switch, or using a manual switch and a relay switch.
- ◆ Long wires: Measure the distance between the two batteries and make sure the wiring in the split-charge kit is long enough.
- ◆ Wire thickness: A high quantity of amps can travel between the vehicle's battery and the leisure battery, so make sure the wires are able to withstand the current. Fuses will prevent too much current being drawn, but make sure a split-charge kit you intend to use is suitable for your batteries.
- ◆ Modern vehicle wiring: If you have a modern camper van, it may be complicated to fit a split-charge system, especially if there are warning systems for a drop in battery voltage. If you are at all unsure about fitting a split-charge system, seek professional advice first.

A split-charge system is more complicated than merely connecting a wire from the vehicle's battery to the leisure battery to transfer power. The recharging must only happen when the vehicle's engine is running to ensure the vehicle's battery is being recharged by the alternator or dynamo, which will in turn provide power to the leisure battery. A switch needs to be fitted between the batteries and most split-

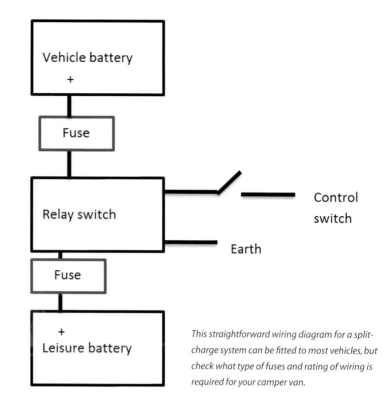

This straightforward wiring diagram for a split-charge system can be fitted to most vehicles, but check what type of fuses and rating of wiring is required for your camper van.

charge systems use a relay switch that is capable of handling the current that will travel through it, whereas using a normal toggle switch could be dangerous. The relay switch can be operated in two ways. It can be operated via a feed from the ignition switch, so whenever the engine is started and run, there will be a live feed to the relay switch and, in turn, the leisure battery will be charged. This involves finding a wire that is only live when the ignition is switched on and routing it to the relay switch. An

additional option is to include a manual switch in this setup, so you can choose to switch off the charging of the leisure battery.

Suitable fuses must be fitted along the wire between the vehicle's battery and the leisure battery to prevent the risk of wires burning out and causing fires. The type of fuse depends on the amount of current that will be drawn and the rating of the wiring.

One of the biggest problems concerning a split-charge system is re-

The relay switch shown here is operated via a live feed from the vehicle, which enables the leisure battery to be charged by the vehicle's battery.

A voltage-sensitive relay (VSR) ensures a leisure battery is only being recharged when the engine is running.

The wiring for a voltage-sensitive relay is straightforward, with connections between the batteries and an earth wire.

charging a flat leisure battery. If the leisure battery's voltage is very low (i.e. it is flat), then the amount of current drawn to recharge it may blow the fuses in the split-charge system. There are a number of solutions to help avoid this problem. One is to check the voltage of the leisure battery and either stop using it when it is low or recharge it using a mains charger. The second option is to use a relay that can control the amount of amps that are delivered to the leisure battery. Providing the wiring and fuses are correctly rated, the leisure battery can then be recharged without damaging anything. This type of relay has an amps rating.

A flat leisure battery can also create problems for starting the vehicle's engine. If the split-charge system is designed to only work when the engine is running, then the very second the ignition is switched on, the leisure battery will start to draw power from the vehicle's battery. If the leisure battery is flat, then it could mean there's no power from the vehicle's battery to turn and start the engine. There are two solutions to this problem. The first is to fit a manual switch (as suggested earlier in this chapter) to operate the relay in the split-charge system. Therefore, the leisure battery cannot be recharged unless the ignition and the switch are on. Another solution is to use a voltage-sensitive relay (VSR). This is a more expensive relay, but only switches over when the voltage supplied to it is usually more than 13.3 volts. So, when the ignition is switched on and the engine is being turned over to start it, the voltage to the relay will be lower than 13 volts because the engine's dynamo or alternator won't be producing elec-

tricity. Consequently, the relay won't switch over and allow the leisure battery to be recharged. When the engine is running and the alternator or dynamo is producing over 13.3 volts, the relay will switch over and allow the leisure battery to be recharged. This type of setup also helps to protect the vehicle's battery from recharging problems caused by the dynamo or alternator.

Connecting a voltage-sensitive relay is quite straightforward. Using suitably thick wiring, run a short wire from the vehicle battery's live terminal to an inline fuse and to the relevant connection on the VSR. Run another suitably thick wire and fuse to the live terminal on the leisure battery. If the VSR has an earth wire, connect this to a suitable location on the vehicle, such as the metal bodywork or a chassis leg.

LIGHTING

There are a number of options for lighting the interior of a camper van, ranging from wind-up and battery-operated torches to LED roof lights. The amount of power consumed by lights is very low, especially by LED or fluorescent lights, so they can often be powered by the leisure battery without the risk of draining it.

Many camping and caravan specialists sell LED and fluorescent strip lights, which can be connected to a 12-volt battery, such as a leisure battery. Some are fitted with a cigarette lighter plug, so they can be fitted to the cigarette lighter socket inside the camper van. However, such lights can also be connected directly to the leisure battery via an inline fuse or fusebox, which is

---

OTHER POWER SOLUTIONS

There are numerous ways to create a source of electricity to power equipment. A roof full of solar panels, for instance, could create sufficient electricity to power some lighting, but would add weight to the camper van and cost a fortune to purchase. A cheaper option would be to use battery-operated LED lighting, which can last for several hours.

A mobile generator can be used to produce electricity for powering main's operated equipment. These usually run on diesel or petrol, so they may not be allowed in a campsite, but can be used elsewhere. Some generators are quiet running, so they won't disturb you (they must be kept outside). Most small, mobile generators provide enough power to recharge equipment and operate a television.

This compact and quiet petrol-driven generator from Machine Mart costs around £100 and produces up to 720 watts of power.

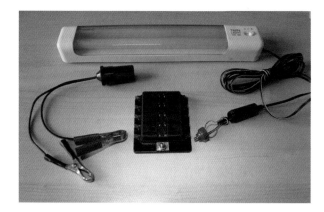

This twin-tube fluorescent light can be connected to a cigarette lighter or adapted to be connected to a leisure battery's fuse box.

explained in greater detail earlier in this chapter. This enables the wiring to be concealed and the light to be made a permanent fixture.

With such a vast range of portable lights to choose from, it's worthwhile buying a number of battery-operated and rechargeable lights and testing them. Many of them are fitted with magnets, so they can be fixed to the inside walls of the camper van. They are often equipped with hooks, so they can be hung in different places around the camper van.

Testing different lighting inside a camper van helps to see where you need it and when you will need it. You may find a head torch is the best equipment for reading a book and a small battery-powered LED light is ideal for low-level lighting when the children have gone to sleep.

Some products work better than others. A battery-operated head torch, for example, is better than a wind-up device when it comes to reading a book. A rechargeable LED worklight may provide more light than a similar light that's powered by AA batteries. Finding out which products work best and where they should be fitted is much easier than installing permanent lighting and discovering it's in the wrong places.

This small and compact LED light is very cheap to buy, is powered by AAA rechargeable batteries and is equipped with a magnet and hook for securing it inside the camper van.

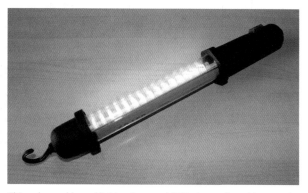

This rechargeable worklight costs around £10 to buy and provides several hours of lighting.

ENTERTAINMENT OPTIONS

There's a wide and seemingly endless range of options for entertainment that can be fitted inside a camper van, which extend beyond a simple stereo head unit and speakers. If you have the budget, then popular equipment includes DVD head units with satellite navigation, roof-mounted televisions, surround sound systems and games consoles. This type of equipment often needs to be professionally installed and can easily cost a four-figure sum.

Some equipment needs to be correctly installed, especially a roof-mounted television screen, which must

Dashboard-mounted stereo head unit with flip-out screen can control all of the entertainment options inside a camper van.

Roof-mounted television can incorporate a DVD player or can be connected to the camper van's stereo or games consoles.

be securely fitted so that it doesn't fall off or tear itself off its mounting points in the event of an accident.

If you are reluctant to spend a lot of money on having the luxury of being able to play games, watch films and listen to music inside your camper van, but still want these options, then there are some cheaper solutions. These include the following:

◆ Stereo solutions: Most simple stereo head units can be connected to a modern digital music player, such as an MP3 player, mobile phone or even a USB memory stick. Old stereo cassette players can use a cassette adapter to connect to an MP3 player or mobile phone. There are also FM transmitters, which allow an MP3 player or similar device

to be connected via the radio of a stereo. The latest entry-level stereos often include a headphone or USB socket, which can be used to connect to a memory stick or digital music player.

◆ Portable amp: If you want to play music inside your camper van, but don't want to fit a stereo with speakers and possibly an amplifier,

Most car stereos can be connected to an MP3 player, mobile phone or memory stick to play music.

A portable amplifier is loud enough for a camper van and much cheaper than buying a car stereo, amplifier and speakers.

then a cheaper approach is to buy a portable amplifier (also known as a portable PA system) for around £80. Many of them can be operated via rechargeable batteries, the vehicle's battery or main electricity. A portable amplifier is loud enough for a camper van and can be connected to devices including MP3 players and mobile phones.

Portable DVD players provide a simple solution to watching films.

◆ Portable DVD player: Often seen strapped to the back of headrests in many family saloons, portable DVD players have a wide range of features and can easily be fitted inside a camper van. Many are powered by the vehicle's battery, their own rechargeable battery or mains electricity, making them ideal for using on the move and when located at a campsite. They can also be connected to other devices, such as a games console.

A laptop provides all round entertainment for a reasonable price.

◆ Laptop: If you want to watch films, backup your photos, check your emails, read e-books, recharge a mobile phone and listen to music, then an entry-level laptop is one of the cheapest solutions. Most laptops can be powered via the camper van's cigarette lighter, as well as mains electricity. The only difficulty concerns securing the laptop when the camper van is moving.

HOW TO FIT AN AMPLIFIER

A sound system inside a camper van can provide all-round entertainment whilst on the move and when camping. It can be used to watch movies, listen to the radio and listen to music. If you are keen to have a good sound quality, then one of the best solutions is to fit an amplifier, which will boost the sound from the stereo, DVD player or whatever device you use, and deliver it to the speakers.

Fitting an amplifier is reasonably straightforward, but there are several safety rules to be aware of. The amplifier needs its own power lead from the battery, which must be fitted with an inline fuse close to its connection on the battery. This is important, because any electrical problems should result in the fuse blowing, but if the wiring to it starts to melt first, then the less wiring there is, the less risk there is of a fire.

The wiring that's connected to an amplifier needs to be separated out between the main power lead and the wires for the speakers. If all of the wires are kept together, the power lead can create interference and distort the sound quality that's running through the speaker wires.

Secure connections are essential in all aspects of fitting an amplifier. The amplifier needs to be securely mounted inside the camper van along with any other components, such as crossovers, a DVD player, stereo head unit and speakers. Similarly, any wiring needs to be securely connected to their respective components using appropriate electrical connectors. Do not use masking tape or electrician's tape to secure electrical

The connections to an amplifier consist of a power lead and speaker wire. Keep these two sets of wires separate to avoid interference.

Make sure all electrical connections are secure to reduce the risk of problems and fires.

- Crimping tool with electrical connectors
- Electrician's tape
- Inline fuse holder and suitable fuse
- Screwdrivers
- Wire (various thickness and colours)

Difficulty level: 3/5
On your own? Yes
Time: 3 hours

connections. Finally, all wires must be securely routed throughout the camper van and taped or strapped down.

The following three step-by-step guides provide general guidance for fitting an amplifier, supplying power to it and routing its wires.

1 Amplifiers need to be kept away from moving parts and water, so choose a location carefully, such as underneath a seat, a floor area or cupboard. Remove any fire hazards, such as polystyrene spacers.
2 Many amplifiers can be fitted vertically on the side of a panel. Make sure there is plenty of room around it to be able to attach cables to it. If the amplifier has mounting lugs on it, use these to secure it with screws or bolts.
3 If you are mounting an amplifier to the floor, make sure it is flat. Trial fit the amplifier to check. If it isn't flat, fit some sound deadening to help level it out and trial fit the amplifier again.
4 Secure the amp with double-sided sticky tape and Araldite. Drilling holes through the floor to mount the amplifier isn't recommended as it runs the risk of water getting into the amplifier and camper van.
5 If you need to fit crossovers to direct the sound from the amplifier to the speakers, these can be fitted near to the amplifier and can be secured with double-sided sticky tape and Araldite.
6 Route the wiring between the amplifier and crossovers. If there are sufficient speaker outputs on the amplifier to power all the speakers, do not use crossovers.

Remove any flammable material from around where the amplifier will be mounted.

Some amplifiers can be fitted to a vertical panel.

Use sound-deadening material to ensure an amplifier is mounted flat on a horizontal surface.

Don't drill through the floor to secure an amplifier, as water may get into it.

Crossovers are useful if you don't have enough outputs on the amplifier for all the speakers.

Route the wiring between the crossovers, amplifier and speakers.

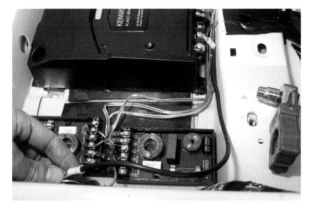

Most amplifiers need earthing to the camper van's bodywork or chassis.

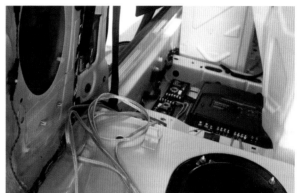

Keep the speaker wires loose until all of them have been installed.

7 The amplifier usually needs to be earthed, so make sure a suitably thick wire is used and connected to a metal part of the camper van's bodywork or chassis.

8 Don't cut or permanently secure any speaker wires to the camper van yet. Leave them loose until all of the wiring has been fitted.

HOW TO POWER AN AMPLIFIER

Most amplifiers are powered by a dedicated lead from the live terminal on the battery. In many cases, this doesn't mean the amplifier is constantly live, because it is switched on and off via the vehicle's stereo. However, the instructions for fitting your own amplifier may be different, so check first. The following two steps explain in general, how most amplifiers are powered.

1 A separate new power lead needs to be fitted direct from the battery to the amplifier. This will be controlled via the stereo head unit and must have an inline fuse (e.g. 30A, but check with your amplifier's fitting instructions).

2 Route the power cable from the previous step down one side of the camper van and keep it away from the wires for the speakers – it can create interference. Secure the cable with tape and make sure it is not near any moving or hot components.

A separate and substantial power lead is required to power the amplifier.

An inline fuse must be fitted close to the power lead's battery terminal.

Keep power cables away from speaker wires to reduce the risk of interference.

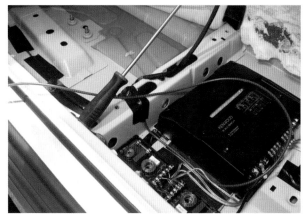

The red wire shown here is the main power cable from the battery to the amplifier.

HOW TO KEEP AMPLIFIER WIRING ORGANIZED

There are a lot of wires connected to an amplifier, so they need to be routed away from moving parts or anything that generates heat. There are also lots of connections that need to be correctly made, including wiring to the speakers and the stereo's head unit. The following steps provide a checklist of what's generally involved.

1   Several wires will need to be connected to the head unit. The speaker outputs will need to be routed to the amplifier. An electrical output will need to be routed to the amplifier to switch it on. In some cases, the wiring may need to be modified.

2   Speaker wires can be routed behind panels or through access holes. Make sure they are kept dry and away from hot or moving parts.

3   Wherever possible, tie wiring together to help reduce the risk of it becoming messy and tangled. Use electrician's tape or cable ties to keep it tidy.

4   Gaffer tape is useful for securing wiring to the body of the camper van. Make sure you won't be standing on these wires and damaging them, even if they are covered by carpet or flooring.

Speaker wires need to be connected between the device for playing music and the amplifier.

Some wires may need to be adapted when connecting a head unit to an amplifier.

Speaker wires can be routed behind or through panels.

Keep wires tidy by tying them together.

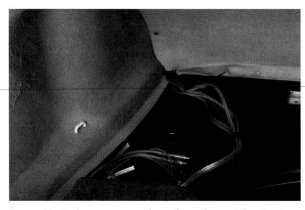

Secure wiring to the camper van with tape, but make sure it doesn't get trapped and damaged.

FITTING A MOBILE COMPRESSOR

Compressed air can be used to inflate a tyre, pump up an air bed or awning or operate air suspension. With the right attachment, it can be even used to dry the dishes!

There are a number of mobile air-compressors that can be installed into a camper van and used for the aforementioned purposes. They are powered by the vehicle's battery or the leisure battery and can be switched on and off via a toggle switch or the engine's ignition switch.

The compressed air that is generated by a compressor can be stored in a tank to help build up and use a reserve of air. Alternatively, it can be used direct from the compressor, although this may mean it takes longer to blow up a bed, for instance, if the compressor has to build up pressure.

The main components required to fit and operate a mobile compressor include

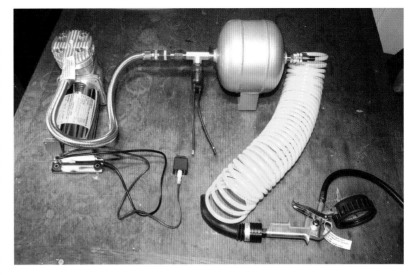

the electrically operated compressor, which uses a piston-operated pump to create compressed air, changing it from normal atmospheric pressure of around 1 bar (14psi) to 8–9 bar (120psi) for a light-duty unit.

When choosing a suitable compressor, consider how much time you will need to use it for and what sort of equipment you intend to use with it. This will help to determine what sort of compressor you need.

COMPRESSOR PARTS

Blow-off valve: Releases air if too much pressure is generated.

Compressor: Electric pump that generates compressed air up to ten times greater than atmospheric pressure.

Connector block: Connects pipework and allows safety equipment, such as a blow-off valve and pressure switch, to be fitted.

Pressure switch: Switches compressor off when a specific pressure is reached in the line or tank.

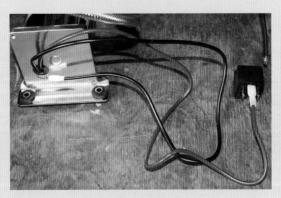

Relay switch: Switches on the compressor and uses an electrical supply from the vehicle's battery or leisure battery.

Tank: Stores compressed air, allowing equipment to be used without having to constantly work the compressor.

Compressors have a duty cycle, which help calculate the amount of time it can be used. For example, if a compressor has a 25 per cent duty cycle, it can be used for say 10 minutes, but will then need to be left for 30 minutes to cool down. More expensive kits have a 100 per cent duty cycle and are ideal for heavy work, such as operating air suspension and air tools.

There are a number of safety features that should be included in a mobile compressor. The air created by a compressor is directed through a pressure switch, which shuts down the compressor when a specific pressure is achieved. Some equipment includes a safety blow-off valve, which will relieve the pressure should it exceed a particular amount.

The steps involved in fitting a mobile compressor are quite straightforward, but it's worthwhile spending just as much time sourcing the right compressor, planning where it should be installed and making sure it is safe. Large components, such as the compressor and tank, can be positioned vertically or horizontally. Electrical connections need to be kept dry and all parts must be protected from moving components. Compressed-air connections should be fitted with PTFE tape to help reduce the risk of air leaks and loose connections, and all pipework must be secured to the vehicle with P-clips or something similar.

Set aside at least half a day to fit a

TOOLBOX

- Crimping tool for electrical connections
- P-clips or similar
- PTFE tape
- Screwdrivers and spanners

Difficulty level: 3/5
On your own? Yes
Time: Half a day

---

mobile compressor. The following steps show an installation of two compressors by Land Rover specialist Matt Savage (01629 55855 www.mattsavage.co.uk), who is the sole UK agent for Viair.

1　Look for a suitable space to fit the compressor. It doesn't need to be near the battery that will be used to operate it. There's plenty of space underneath the passenger seat illustrated.

2　Make sure the location for mounting the compressor is dry and there's space to fit all the connections to it. Secure the compressor so it won't move around when the vehicle is being driven. There are two compressors being fitted here and they are mounted on a wooden board.

3　The electrical supply to the compressor needs an earth. Look for the earth lead attached to the compressor and secure it to a metal part of the chassis or bodywork using a nut and bolt.

4　The compressor must be activated via a relay, not a direct supply from a battery. The relay can be switched via an ignition-live lead or a manual switch. There are two relays shown here because two compressors are being fitted.

5　Secure a pressure switch, safety blow-off valve and two air-line connections to a four-way connector block. The air generated by the compressor will pass through this block and be monitored by the switch and valve.

6　Fit the four-way connector block to a secure position on the vehicle using suitable mounts or P-clips. Route earth wires from the relay(s) via the pressure switch and to a metal part of the chassis or bodywork.

7　Mount an air outlet that can be used to connect equipment and make use of the compressed air. Make sure the outlet is easy to access and any equipment that is connected can be used (e.g. an air-line for inflating tyres will stretch to all of the wheels).

Find a suitable, dry location to store the compressor, such as underneath a seat or inside a low-level cupboard.

Securely mount the compressor. There are two compressors being fitted here.

Make sure the earth wire from the compressor is secured to a metal part of the body or chassis of the camper van.

The compressor is powered and activated via a relay switch – there are two here for two compressors.

A connector block is used to fit a pressure switch and blow-off valve.

The pressure switch at the top will cut the earth from the relay switches if the air pressure is too much.

8 Fit suitable pipework between the outlet on the compressor and the connector block fitted in step 6. Use PTFE tape for an airtight connection. The outlets from two compressors shown here are fed into a T-piece, which leads to the connector block.

9 Route pipework from the one remaining outlet on the connector block to the storage tank and/or the air outlet that was fitted in step

7. Secure all pipework with P-clips to prevent connections becoming loose or damaged.

10 If you intend to fit a tank, secure it in a safe location, such as underneath the vehicle. Route the pipework from the last step to the tank(s) and make sure the connection is secure by using PTFE tape.

11 Route a power supply from the battery to the air compressor's relay that was fitted in step 4.

Include a suitable inline fuse close to the connection to the battery. There are two wires shown here for the two relays that control two compressors.

12 Check that all wiring and pipework are secure and there are no loose electrical connections. Switch on the compressor and operate some equipment (e.g. inflate a tyre), then recheck all fittings to make sure everything is secure.

Mount an easy-to-access outlet to connect equipment such as an air line to inflate a bed.

Pipework from the compressor must be airtight, so use PTFE tape on threaded connections.

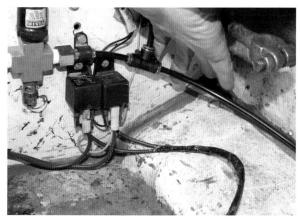

The compressed air is directed through the connector block on the left, then onto an outlet and a tank.

Tanks can be used to store compressed air and operate equipment for longer periods of time.

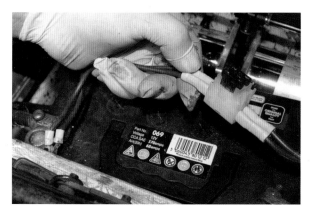

An inline fuse must be used for the main power feed from the battery to the air compressor.

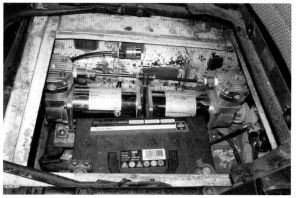

A completed installation using two compressors.

expanding a camper van

The space inside a camper van can be restrictive, but there's nothing to stop you extending it through awnings, pop-tops and high-tops.

HOW TO MAKE YOUR OWN CANOPY

Professional canopies can be expensive, but if all you need is some additional cover to keep you dry or to create extra shade, then a simple cover can be erected using cheap-to-buy tarpaulin, a few poles used for tent porches, some string and a handful of tent pegs.

A large tarpaulin can be bought from most camping shops for a fraction of the cost of a canopy. Whilst it's usually used as a ground sheet, and thus has a number of eyelets around the edges, this makes it ideal for a shelter. The eyelets can be used to tie down the tarpaulin and support it with tent poles that are used for a porch.

There are a number of disadvantages to the DIY approach outlined here. First, the results are never going to look as good as a professional awning, but you will have saved a lot of money. Second, be prepared to experiment with the layout and structure of your DIY awning to ensure it can withstand wind and rain. In particular, rain water may collect and make the awning sag, so you will have to look at different methods of draining off the unwanted water and arranging the poles.

The following steps outline a general guide to making your own canopy.

A professionally made canopy has all the luxuries of easy operation and a reliable shelter, but they are expensive to buy.

TOOLBOX

- Rubber mallet
- String or guy ropes
- Tarpaulin
- Tent pegs

Difficulty level: 1/5
On your own? Easier with a second pair of hands
Time: 30 minutes

1   Position your camper van with plenty of space around it so you can experiment with the awning. Lay the tarpaulin on the ground and fit two or four tent poles together. Use poles with a slim spike at the end, which can fit through the eyelets in the tarpaulin.

2   Support one corner of the tarpaulin with a tent pole and tie it down with at least two lengths of string or two guy ropes. The poles may fall over, so ask a few people to help hold them up, if necessary.

3   Attach some string or rope to the edges of the tarpaulin that are closest to your camper van. Pull the string or rope across the roof of the camper van, making sure some of the tarpaulin covers the roof. Secure this to the ground or the camper van.

4   The tarpaulin can sag in the middle, which will form a collection point for rainwater and limits the headroom underneath. You may need to fit additional poles or alter the height of existing ones to avoid this problem.

5   When you want to move the camper van but leave the awning in position, detach the side where it's connected to the camper van and tie it down to the ground – this will help to keep the awning secure and freestanding.

6   This cheap DIY canopy can be erected in a number of different ways. It doesn't have to be attached to the camper van and can be secured next to it, if required. If there are any trees nearby, these can be used to tie ropes to.

Make sure you have plenty of room around your camper van to experiment with different layouts for your homemade awning.

Starting with one tent pole, secure it upright with a couple of lengths of string or rope.

Attach rope or string to the eyelets in the tarpaulin, then stretch them over the roof of the camper van.

The tarpaulin may sag in places, which will collect rainwater, so adjust the poles to eliminate this problem.

The tarpaulin can be detached from the camper van and secured to the ground to make it free standing.

This type of canopy can be left free standing and doesn't need to be attached to the camper van.

FITTING AN AWNING

An awning is simply a tent attached to the side of the camper van. Many of them have the advantage of being free-standing and the fact that the camper van can be driven away without having to undo any ropes (known as a drive away awning). However, this luxury often comes at a price, so most awnings are much more expensive than equivalent tents. Consequently, some people have adapted a tent to act as an awning, using waterproof fabric to fit between the tent and camper van.

Fitting an awning on to a camper van is usually very easy, but the work involved depends on the type of awning you are using. The following steps provide a general overview of what's involved.

A normal tent can be used as a type of awning. The green fabric between the tent and camper van seen here connects the two together.

1 Layout the contents of the awning. There will probably be several poles, which need to be attached to create a framework. Assemble these and, if necessary, feed them through any holes in the awning's cover.

2 Pull the framework into position and the awning will start to take shape. In some cases, the outer cover is hooked into the framework.

3 Once the awning has been constructed, it can be moved into position. Move it close to the camper van's side door. Extra people may be required to help here.

4 Find any ropes that help to secure the awning to the camper van. Depending on the type of awning

Most awnings consist of a metal framework, which needs to be assembled.

Feed the poles through the awning's outer cover. This will form a framework to erect the awning.

you have, the method of attaching it to the camper van may be different.

5　If the awning needs to be attached to the camper van, look for a suit-able point to tie straps or ropes to it. Make sure the paintwork won't get damaged.

6　Most awnings offer a variety of configurations, so you can experi-ment with different doors and lay-outs. Keep checking that the awn-ing remains sturdy and leak-free, adjusting the structure and straps, if necessary.

Look for hooks and straps to attach the awning's cover to the framework.

Carry or drag the constructed awning so that it is positioned next to the camper van's side door.

Locate any ropes or straps that attach the awning to the side of the camper van.

Attach the awning's straps to the camper van, making sure they won't damage the paintwork.

One of the many benefits of an awning is having sheltered access to the camper van and an additional area undercover.

The awning may need adjusting, especially when it rains and water gets trapped on the roof.

HOW TO FIT AN ELEVATING ROOF

One of the best ways to create more space inside a camper van is to fit an elevating roof, which is also known as a pop-top. There are a number of manufacturers of such roofs with a variety of different designs. One of the most popular is a GRP roof (general reinforced plastic, commonly known as fibreglass) consisting of hinges at one end and gas rams at the other. Different designs have the hinges at the front, rear or sides, which provide space for sleeping compartments and extra headroom.

Fitting an elevating roof to a camper van isn't as straightforward as it may seem. It's not just a case of cutting a hole in the roof, laying the new elevating roof in position and fitting some hinges. The roof needs to be strengthened to replace the rigid structure it had before a hole was cut in it. This usually involves fitting strengthening beams around the hole and in positions where the camper van's original strengthening beams were located. Consequently, most of the camper van's headlining and trim needs to be discarded, modified or renewed.

The following steps shows how VW T4 and T5 specialist T4 Transformations of Wakefield in West Yorkshire (01924 339004 www.t4transformations.co.uk) fit an elevating roof from Pop-top Roofs (www.poptoproofs.co.uk) to a VW T5.

Cutting Out the Roof

1   The headlining inside the van needs to be removed to make sure there are no wires that could be cut through when cutting a hole in the roof. Headlining is usually glued in position, or secured with clips or screws.

2   From inside the cab, the headlining and the trim down the pillars may need to be removed to be able to secure any strengthening beams or to cut through the roof. It's best to remove trim that could be damaged from grinding sparks when cutting the roof.

The headlining needs to be removed to see if any wires will be damaged when cutting a hole in the roof.

The headlining in the cab needs to be removed to be able to fit a strengthening beam.

Even the trim down the A-pillars needs to be removed. It helps to protect it from grinding sparks when cutting out the roof.

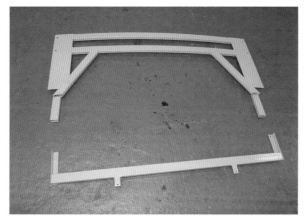

The front strengthening beam is at the top of the photograph and the rear is at the bottom.

These are the side strengthening beams, which need to be trimmed to length.

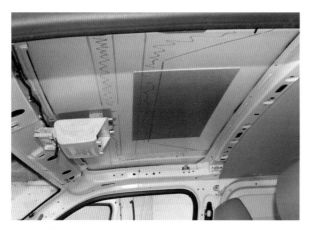

After trial fitting and marking the location of the front strengthening beam, it's easy to see where it needs to be located.

With the location of the front strengthening beam marked, holes can be drilled through to the outside to help show where to cut out the roof.

3 Most elevating-roof conversions use strengthening beams to replace the rigidity the roof provided. With the roof cut away, strength needs to be put back in somehow and most conversions use beams at the front, rear and sides.

4 In some cases, a strengthening beam needs to be trial fitted and its position marked to be able to drill mounting holes or mark areas of the roof for cutting out. Drilling holes from the underside through the roof shows where to cut the roof on top.

5 Once the position of at least one strengthening beam is determined, the top of the van's roof can be marked to show where to cut it out. The roof will be cut to specific dimensions and in particular areas.

6 Before cutting the roof, it's important to protect the upholstery, trim and glass of the van. Grinding sparks and shards of metal generated from cutting the roof will damage them, so refit the headlining and use lots of old bed sheets and rags to protect everything from the door mirrors to the windscreen.

7 Using an angle grinder with a cutting disc, a hole is cut in the roof to specific dimensions. Only the outer

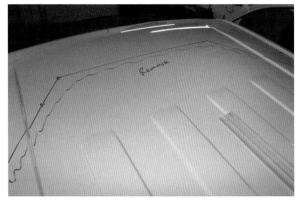

Measured markings on the top of the roof show where it will be cut.

Protect glass and upholstery with thick blankets or cardboard. Sparks from cutting with an angle grinder could damage them or start a fire.

An angle grinder with cutting disc can be used to cut the outer skin of the roof.

The outer skin of the roof can be removed after it has been cut.

These strengthening beams need to be cut before fitting the elevating roof.

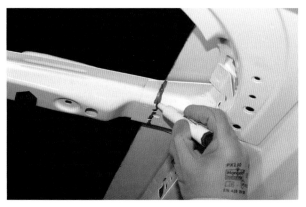

Mark across the strengthening beams to see where they should be cut.

An angle grinder with a cutting disc can be used to cut through the strengthening beams.

A jigsaw with a long metal blade can cut the strengthening beams where space is tight, such as a corner.

skin of the roof is cut away, leaving the standard strengthening beams in position, so it is safe to stand on the roof when cutting through it.

8   After cutting all the way round the roof, the cut out panel can be peeled away. In most cases, there will be roof-strengthening beams underneath the roof, which won't have been cut through.

9   Any strengthening beams that run across the hole in the roof need to be cut out. First, it's wise to mark where to cut, using the existing lines where the roof has been cut. This helps to ensure a neat cut is made.

10 The beams are cut away using an angle grinder and cutting disc, or a jigsaw and a long blade. In some cases, a jigsaw is easier, especially in tight corners where an angle grinder and cutting disc are awkward to manoeuvre into position.

11 Once all the cutting of the roof is complete, the cut edges will be sharp and, despite the fact they will be covered, it's best to make them smooth with a file and to paint them to prevent corrosion.

12 Any wiring that originally runs along the roof should be cable tied or repositioned. Wires that are routed to roof-mounted lighting can be reused, providing mounting holes are made for the lights.

Fitting the Strengthening Beams

1   All of the strengthening beams are secured to the camper van using silicone-based adhesive (e.g. Sikaflex) and pop rivets. The silicone helps to reduce panel rattle. The rear strengthening beam is fitted first. The roof panel is painted where the beam will sit to help the silicone stick.

2   The rear strengthening beam is secured with pop rivets fitted at 15cm intervals. A series of 5mm holes are drilled through the roof panel and beam before fitting the pop rivets. The beam is fitted across the rear of the roof.

3   The front strengthening beam is secured in exactly the same way as the rear beam. It's more involved because it's larger, so needs to be fitted with more pop rivets and

File the cut edges around the hole that has been cut out.

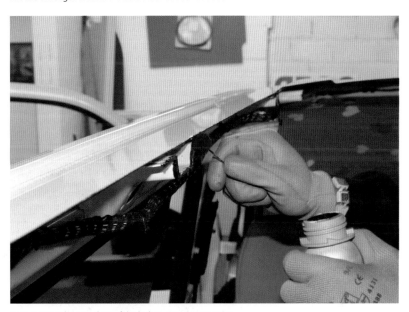

Rust-protect the cut edges of the hole to prevent corrosion.

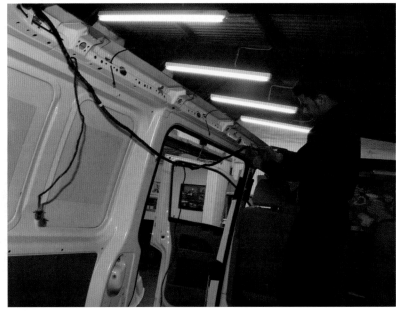

Route any roof wires and secure them with cable ties.

covers most of the remainder of the underside of the roof in the cab area.

4   With the front and rear strengthening beams fitted, there are two side beams to fit next. These resemble sills and need to be trimmed to fit. They are made of steel and provide the strength in the van's shell that has been lost through cutting out the roof.

5   Plenty of silicone is applied along the side edges of the hole in the roof prior to fitting the side strengthening beams. This helps to insulate the old and new metal panels and reduce the risk of squeaks and rattles.

6   The side strengthening beams are carefully moved into position, then 5mm holes are drilled at each end through them and the van's roof, before pop rivets are fitted. Holes are drilled at 15cm intervals along the top and underside to locate more pop rivets.

Silicone-based adhesive is applied to the strengthening beams to help them stick when fitted.

More silicone-based adhesive is added to the underside of the roof where the strengthening beams are fitted.

The rear strengthening beam is secured with pop rivets, as well as silicone-based adhesive.

The front strengthening beam is larger than the rear and is also secured with pop rivets.

Two sill-shaped strengthening beams are trimmed to length before being fitted down the sides of the camper van's remaining roof.

More silicone-based adhesive is used to fit the side strengthening beams. This helps to reduce the risk or squeaks and rattles.

Holes are drilled along the top of the remaining roof and through the side strengthening beams before fitting pop rivets.

Holes are also drilled from underneath the strengthening beams to fit more pop rivets.

Fitting the Elevating Roof

1   With the strengthening for the elevating roof complete, the sides of the inside of the van can be trimmed in carpet. The carpeting can extend up to and over the side strengthening beams.

2   The elevating roof is trial fitted, measured and marked to show its position on the van. This helps to determine the exact position of the hinges, which need to be fixed to the top of the roof.

3   With the position of the roof marked, the mounting holes for its hinges can be measured and drilled. This particular elevating roof has hinges at the rear and gas rams at the front, which are supplied fixed to the underside of the new GRP roof.

4   The gas rams at the front of the elevating roof are each secured to the top of the van with a knuckle. The knuckle has two mounting holes. Existing threaded holes along the guttering can be used, or new ones created with rivet nuts.

5   When all the mounting points have been drilled for the elevating roof, the roof can be lifted back into position on the top of the van and the rear hinges secured. The roof needs to be raised using tall jacks to allow access to mounting the hinges to the top of the van.

6   Connecting the gas ram to its knuckle, which is mounted on the roof gutter of the van, requires the front of the roof to be raised, making sure at the same time that

The inside of the camper van can now be lined right up to the strengthening beams.

The elevating roof is lifted into position to measure its position.

there's enough clearance (unless you're working out-side).

7   A strip of plastic trim is used to secure the elevating roof's canvas sides along the top of the van's roof. These need to be cut to size and trimmed further to ensure they can tuck under the side strengthening beams.

8   The plastic trim used to secure the canvas sides of the elevating roof are secured with a series of screws, which allows adjustment to ensure the sides are taut when the roof is raised. When a good fit is achieved, the trim is glued and tidied up with a bead of sealant.

The mounting holes for the roof's hinges are drilled.

Sometimes, existing holes can be used to mount components. Here, threaded holes are being used to mount the knuckles for the roof's gas rams.

The roof is refitted and the hinges fitted in position.

The hinges are mounted at the rear of the roof and in this case, are pre-fitted to the underside of the GRP.

The gas rams at the front of the elevating roof are fixed to their locating knuckles.

Plastic trim is used to secure the canvas sides of the elevating roof.

The plastic trim that secures the roof's canvas sides is fitted with screws and glue.

HOW TO FIT A HIGH-TOP ROOF

Another solution to raising the headroom inside a camper van is to fit a high-top. Some vans, such as the Mercedes Sprinter and Ford Transit, are available in high-top versions as standard, where there is sufficient headroom inside the rear to be able to stand up. However, there are a number of aftermarket high-top conversions available, which involve fitting strengthening beams to the underside of the roof, cutting a large hole in the roof and fixing a higher GRP roof on top.

The steps involved in fitting a high-top are similar in many ways to fitting a pop-top, which is covered in the previous section. So the following steps provide an overview of what's involved.

1 Most high-tops are constructed from GRP and made from a mould. They are usually supplied with a white gel coat finish and will need to be lined on the inside with carpeting or a similar material.
2 Strengthening beams should be fitted to keep the upper-half of the van's bodywork rigid. Depending on the conversion, this may be fitted before or after the roof has been cut out.
3 The roof is cut out in the same way as fitting a pop-top, using an angle grinder or jigsaw. The cut edges are smoothed over with a file and paint protected to prevent corrosion.
4 Once the roof has been cut and the strengthening beams fitted, the new GRP roof is lifted onto the top of the van and secured with a bonding sealant.

Not enough room to stand up in a van? A high-top roof conversion is one solution.

5 The inside of the roof needs to be lined with carpet or a similar material to prevent condensation and to isolate the fibreglass material of the roof.

6 With a fixed roof, there's room to permanently fit cupboards and other methods of storage. Brackets can also be fitted to add solid beds or hammocks.

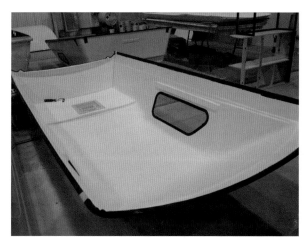

GRP high-tops can include windows and air vents.

Most high-top roofs are made from GRP using a mould.

Strengthening beams are fitted to the underside of the van's roof to keep it rigid.

A Transit van with its roof cut and ready for fitting a GRP high-top.

A GRP high-top roof isn't heavy, but requires a few people to carefully manoeuvre it onto the top of a van.

The inside of the GRP roof must be lined to seal the fibreglass and keep condensation away.

A fixed roof provides more storage space in the form of cupboards and lockers.

HOW TO FIT SIDE WINDOWS

If you are converting a panel van into a camper van, then you will probably want some additional side windows. There are a number of ways of adding windows, but most of them involve cutting out a hole in the side of the van and either inserting a piece of glass or Perspex, or securing something over the hole. Inserting a piece of glass or Perspex into the hole is difficult: first, you have to make sure the hole that is cut out is accurate and, second, the glass or Perspex will need to be held tight with a rubber seal. The easier approach is to secure a piece of glass or Perspex that is larger than the hole. It can be secured to the bodywork around the hole for the window using a variety of materials including silicone and in the case of Perspex, small nuts and bolts.

The following steps outline what's involved in measuring and cutting out a hole in the side of a van and securing a piece of glass to the exterior. The glass shown is specially made and follows the curvature of the van in the photographs (a VW T5 Transporter). All of the work shown was completed at T4 Transformations of Wakefield in West Yorkshire (01924 339004; www.t4transformations. co.uk).

Cutting through metal panels can be

fiddly and potentially dangerous if you use the wrong tools. One of the best tools for the job is known as a nibbler, which is purposely designed to cut through sheet metal. Air-fed nibblers can quickly cut through sheet metal, although there are other types, including hand-operated nibblers and even a sort of nibbler that attaches to the end of an electric hand-drill. Similar tools for cutting through sheet metal include a jigsaw and angle grinder with cutting disc. Wear safety goggles, gloves and ear defenders when operating this type of equipment.

TOOLBOX

- Angle grinder, nibbler or jigsaw
- File
- Goggles, gloves and ear-defenders
- Primer, rust protection and paint
- Sealant

Difficulty level: 5/5
On your own? Extra help required at times
Time: 2–3 hours

Tools such as a jigsaw can be used to cut a window out. Make sure you protect your eyes with goggles or a visor.

Remove any trim from around the area that needs to be cut.

Use a marker pen to calculate where to cut a hole for the window.

Drilling holes through the side of the van helps to transfer the measurements for the hole.

1. Inspect both sides of the panel where you intend to fit a window. This will help to determine how it is going to be cut out and what tools you will need. Remove any trim that will get in the way when cutting and fitting the window.

2. Mark the area that needs to be cut. Start on one side (inside or outside), depending on whether you can identify a specific area to cut out. The markings can be transferred to the other side in the next step.

3. Drill a series of holes through the edges of the area you intend to cut for the window. This will help to transfer the markings made on one side through to the other side. You may need to drill several holes to ensure the markings are accurately transferred.

4. Move to the other side of the panel for the window and mark the area that needs to be cut. This will help to see whether the resulting window is in the correct position both on the inside and outside of the camper van.

5. Carefully cut round the marked area for the window. If you are using a nibbler, the debris from cutting can be very sharp, so try removing it with a vacuum cleaner whilst cutting. Try cutting out the hole in sections if it's awkward.

6 Some sections may need to be cut with an angle grinder and cutting disc, such as a strengthening beam. Make sure all upholstery and glass is protected from grinding sparks – lay blankets and sheets over them.

7 When you are approaching the end of cutting out the panel for the window, ask someone to hold the panel to prevent it falling and damaging something. Use a file to smooth the cut edges and paint them to prevent corrosion.

8 Before fitting the window, you may want to upholster around the inside panel and secure any trim over the edges where the hole has been cut. This will help to achieve a neat and tidy finish.

9 This window conversion requires glass to be secured to the outside of the van. It will be secured with sealant, but first the area where the sealant is going to be applied needs to be keyed to make sure it sticks. This can be done by rubbing it down and painting it with a suitable primer.

10 The sealant that is used to secure the glass to the side of the van is applied with a gun. The nozzle on the end of the canister is cut at a 45-degree angle to ensure a thick ridge of sealant is applied all the way round the hole.

Transfer the measurements to the outside of the van to double check the window will be in the correct position.

Cut out the hole for the window. Here an air-fed nibbler is being used with a vacuum cleaner to remove the debris.

Strengthening panels can be removed using an angle grinder and cutting disc.

11 Four lengths of masking tape are fitted to the edges of the glass or around the edges of the hole. These will help to keep the window in position when it's initially fitted, although they won't be able to hold the window on their own – the sealant must do this.

12 The glass is carefully positioned on the exterior of the van, making sure it covers the hole and is lined up correctly. It may slip down at first, so the masking tape is firmly pushed over it to help secure it in position. The sealant is left to dry before removing the masking tape.

When the panel has almost been cut out, ask someone to hold it, so that it doesn't fall and damage the bodywork.

Trim inside the van before fitting the window. Carpet can be fitted over the edges of the hole for a neat finish.

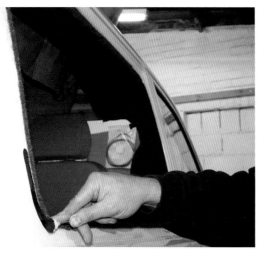

Primer is applied around the edges of the hole to help the sealant for the glass to stick to the van.

The sealant that secures the glass is applied all the way round the hole.

Masking tape helps to initially locate the glass and is either fitted to the edges of the glass or around the hole.

Once the window is in position, allow the sealant to dry before driving the van.

EXTERIOR ACCESSORIES

The limitations of space inside a camper van means that some features have to be fitted outside. Whilst it's possible to fit a shower inside a camper van, it's not really practical and the space taken up could be used for other purposes. However, that doesn't mean to say a shower cannot be fitted to the exterior of the camper van.

Leisure Hubs of Birmingham (0121 753 6800; www.leisurehubs.com) have developed a hot-shower system that is fitted to the tailgate. Known as a surf shower, it is mounted in the back panel

of the tailgate and is operated when the tailgate is raised.

With hot running water courtesy of a Webasto diesel-powered heater, the Leisure Hubs surf shower is extremely versatile, not only allowing the whole family to wash in privacy (when fixed with a wrap-around shower curtain or Pack a Shack Awning) but also a place to wash camping equipment, bikes, surf boards, even pets, keeping your interior free of muddy paw prints.

Fix a wrap-around shower curtain or a Pack A Shack awning to the tailgate and the surf shower can be used by all the family.

Exterior showers can be relatively simple, consisting of a shower hose and head connected to a water pump and warm or cold water tank. Camping accessory manufacturers such as Hi Gear produce a portable shower, which consists of a water bag, hose and shower head. The water is stored in the 20-litre bag and should be left out in the sun to warm up. The bag needs to be suspended above head height for a shower. Don't expect boiling hot water, but in the right climate, it will be warm enough for a shower, or can be used to wash the dishes.

This tailgate awning from Pack A Shack can be used with the surf shower from Leisure Hubs to create an enclosed washroom.

Shower head and hose can be used to rinse down after a day at the beach.

This surf shower from Leisure Hubs makes use of the tailgate and provides hot water from a Webasto diesel-powered heater.

index

RELATED TITLES FROM CROWOOD

Classic Dormobile Camper Vans
MARTIN WATTS
ISBN 978 1 84797 083 1
128pp, over 300 illustrations

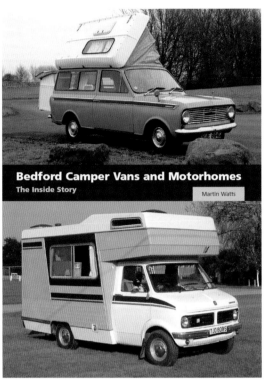

Bedford Camper Vans and Motorhomes
MARTIN WATTS
ISBN 978 1 84797 157 9
160pp, over 200 illustrations

VW Camper – The Inside Story
DAVE ECCLES
ISBN 978 1 84797 417 4
192pp, over 500 illustrations

VW Camper – Inspirational Interiors
DAVE ECCLES
ISBN 978 1 84797 070 1
224pp, over 400 illustrations

Volkswagen T3
RICHARD COPPING
ISBN 978 1 84797 239 2
128pp, over 200 illustrations

Volkswagen T4
RICHARD COPPING
ISBN 978 1 84797 554 6
208pp, over 350 illustrations

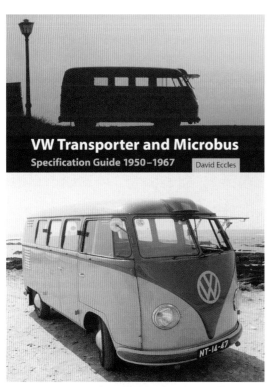

**VW Transporter and Microbus Specification
Guide 1950–1967**
DAVE ECCLES
ISBN 978 1 86126 652 1
96pp, over 400 illustrations

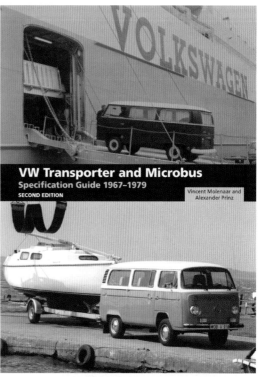

**VW Transporter and Microbus Specification
Guide 1967–1979**
VINCENT MOLENAAR & ALEXANDER PRINZ
ISBN 978 1 84797 480 8
128pp, over 450 illustrations

In case of difficulty ordering, please contact the Sales Office:

The Crowood Press Ltd, Ramsbury, Wiltshire SN8 2HR UK

Tel: 44 (0) 1672 520320   enquiries@crowood.com   www.crowood.com